I THOUGHT WE HAD YEARS

HAD YEARS

A Daughter's Story

Lauren Love

I Thought We Had Years

Copyright @ 2022 Lauren Love

The right of Lauren Love to be identified as the Author of
the work has been asserted by her in accordance with the
Copyright, Designs and Patents Act 1988.

No part of this book may be reproduced in any form,
by photocopying or by any electronic or mechanical means,
including information storage or retrieval systems,
without permission in writing from both the copyright
owner and the publisher of this book.

ISBN Number 9798364332769

First Published in 2022
By Amazon Kindle Direct Publishing

For Bernadette

Lauren Love

Table of Contents

I Thought We Had Years

I Thought We Had Years

Lauren Love

Lauren Love

The Notebooks

I have started this book several times in the last three years, worrying about my writing style, whether it was more about me than it was about mom, Bernadette. Some days unable to think, let alone write, through the overwhelming grief … those days were many, so many that I didn't write at all for over twelve months.

Mom kept her heartbreaks and struggles hidden. She used the written word as an outlet in notebooks I found after she died. Each entry signed "B" for Bernadette. The first time I read them I sobbed so hard I could hardly breath. The second, third, maybe fourth time I cried, digesting her thoughts, her feelings. I didn't look at them at all for a long time. The next time I did, these words jumped out at me,

"Eugene* says everyone has a book inside them waiting to come out. He may be right! B" * Bernadette's nephew

I Thought We Had Years

The seed was sown, I wanted to tell mom's story. I tried but struggled. Then whilst reading a book in bed one night, a line in it stopped me in my tracks … 'Those we love never die, not really, not if we remember them well enough. If we stop mourning them and start listening to them, they can, in short, be our saviour.' The next day I began to heal, I began to listen, I began to write, Bernadette's story, my story, our story, told together, the only way it ever could be.

Lauren Love

A Round of Applause

When I was at school, I used to write mom poems. She had kept every single one in a deep red, hexagonal box, in her bedroom. When I was in my forties, she handed me a wrapped gift. It was not my birthday or Christmas but that was not unusual, she would often give me gifts, always wrapped with a bow. It was a blank notebook. On the inside cover she had written,

"For Poetry only, by strictest order, Mom x"

It was a nod towards a shared memory when we went to the cinema in 1984 to see 'Educating Rita.' Rita bought her Tutor, with whom she had struck up a special friendship, a pen, with the same inscription. I was taken back to the girl I used to be before life became busy, before routine set in. Mom had a way of gently taking me by the hand as she stopped to smell the roses.

And so, I began to write poems again. For her seventieth birthday I wrote a poem called 'A Round of applause.' I rolled it into a scroll, tied a bright pink ribbon around it, placed it into a rectangular bright pink sparkly box and smiled to myself as I finished it with a big bright pink bow on top. She kept it on her bedside table for the next seventeen calendar months to the day she died.

Round of Applause

I can see you're happy now,
Happier, I think, than you've ever been
And it makes me smile inside
It's more than I dared to dream.
*

Keeping 'Busy Doing Nothing',
Your favourite way to spend the day,
But everything must stop,
For 'Neighbours' and 'Home and Away'
*

Stopping to smell the lilac tree in the Grove,
Adopting the latest Asda Gnome,
Keeping Christmas lights on all year round,
A taste for travel, but 'There's No Place Like Home.'
*

You always know what someone needs.
A torch, a lighter, a nail file or pen,
Not for Christmas or Birthdays,
Just because you were thinking of them.
*

Buying me notebooks *"For Poetry Only,
By Strictest Order, Mom"*
Putting family first and never having favourites,
Umm … one word … Tom! *

Lauren Love

*

Lighting up everyone's life.
Our world without you would be one long power cut,
I look forward to our daily chats on the phone,
Just to check "What's afoot?"

*

I hope I see the world through your eyes,
Life is more fun alongside you,
With your sense of mischief
And your rose-tinted view.

*

As you think I put Pam Ayres to shame
(Not biased of course!),
I've put pen to paper,
Because you are One in A Million,
And this is your Round of Applause.

* Bernadette's nephew whom she had a soft spot for.

I am so glad I wrote that poem. Mom was over the moon
 as she showed it to her sister Patricia.

"How does she know you stop to smell the lilac tree in the grove?" Patricia asked.

"She knows everything" mom said beaming with pride. I wanted her to know how special she was because she never thought she was at all. I wanted her to realise how far she had come from those days of making do, financially and emotionally with dad. I had to tell her how much joy she brought to others. I wished for a better life for her with all my heart and here she was finally happy. She soaked up every drop of that happiness, knowing more than most, just how precious it was. Her quiet strength and limitless capacity for love had brought her here, despite so much.

Lauren Love

The Unbreakable Bond

Winter stubbornly hung in the air though it was the first month of spring. Bernadette looked nervous as she took one last look in the mirror. She had a timeless, classic look about her with a chestnut Mary Quant style bob that sat just above her slim shoulders. Her jade green knee length woollen coat was buttoned up. The coat had an unusual stand up, square neckline, chequered jade and yellow. Peeping out two inches below the hemline, was a matching chequered dress. As she slipped her feet into jade court shoes, there was a light knock on the bedroom door as her mom stepped in. Lucy stood in the doorway in a black woollen skirt suit with ice blue piping around the edges matching her shimmering ice blue, high neck blouse. The deep black of the suit perfectly mirroring the colour of her short, full fringed hair.

"Oh, you look beautiful Bernadette." Lucy stopped in her tracks as she admired her youngest daughter, who had barely turned nineteen. Bernadette looked over her shoulder and smiled nervously at her mom. She was not fidgeting or repeatedly straightening her outfit or hair as many a young girl on her wedding day might. But when Lucy looked in her daughter's eyes, she knew as mothers always do.

"I'm not sure I should marry him" Bernadette confided.

"If you have any doubt, any at all, then you should not go through with this bab. You know we will look after you and the baby." Lucy's strength was unwavering, but no more was said as they went downstairs. In the kitchen her dad, Henry, was still ashen looking, his complexion paler than his baby blonde hair. He had been this way since she had broken the news of her pregnancy a few months before. He had literally lost his voice worrying what the neighbours would say if their daughter had a child out of wedlock. She had overheard her mom and dad talking many a night after they had gone to bed. Lucy would defy the world for her two girls and Bernadette knew she had meant every word she said. But it was 1967 and not the done thing. Bernadette felt her dad's disappointment and couldn't bear to make matters worse. She worried that it would make him unwell.

By one o'clock she was stood outside Birmingham Registry office with confetti in her hair. Next to her stood Derek, still just eighteen, but a look of early twenties about him. The smile on his handsome face never reached his eyes. He slipped his arm loosely around his new wife's waist, standing sure footed in a mid-grey drainpipe suit, white shirt and black tie. She knew he must have had the same doubts. He had no idea of hers.

They lived with Lucy, Henry, and Patricia while they saved for a place of their own. Less than four months later their son Ben was born. Bernadette doted on him; he was the most precious thing in the world to her.

"When you were tiny I wouldn't put you to bed like mom said I should because I couldn't let you out of my sight for one second. You were so precious, and I thought you couldn't be trusted to look after yourself on your own in your cot upstairs away from me. They didn't have intercoms in 1967! So you had to stay up with me with the telly softly in the background and a soft light on. B"

A few months later they had moved into their own flat. It wasn't easy for either of them, they were still teenagers with a baby. Bernadette's reluctance to marry had not been because she didn't love Derek, she did. It was something deeper in her gut, something that made her uncertain of him, uncertain if he loved her. Derek would work during the week and go out drinking with his mates most nights.

One snowy winter's night, well past midnight , Bernadette was mad that he was out so late again, so she locked the front door. Derek was furious when he returned, he smashed the window to get in. Bernadette was stood in her nightdress holding her crying baby in her arms. Derek grabbed her and threw them both outside in three-inch-deep snow. Bernadette looked down at her bare feet, wrapped Ben's blanket tightly around him and walked three quarters of a mile to her auntie May's house. She never stood up to him again after that night.

Over the next two years, Bernadette felt her happiness and her identity slipping away. She felt invisible, unheard, and worthless. When Ben was an energetic, blonde, three-year-old, Bernadette left Derek and moved back to her parent's house. But Ben missed his dad and kept asking his mom when they were going home. So, when Derek turned up asking her to return, she did for her son's sake. Once again ignoring her gut.

Soon after, she told Derek she wanted another baby. Here's where I come in. All tucked up in the foetal position, feeling her heartbeat. Already wanted, already loved, already needed. The unbreakable bond already formed.

Lauren Love

The Breakdown

M om thought I was beautiful when I was born, just perfect and that's how she made me feel every day for the rest of my life. She doted on me and Ben, we were her world. But as time went on her sense of self-worth diminished more and more.

Lucy and Henry were school caretakers. When an evening cleaning job became available at the school, their daughters took it. Both Patricia and mom were now married with two young children so Lucy and Henry would look after us kids while their daughters cleaned for two hours each evening. Mom opened a post office account and paid her wages into it. It wasn't much but she wanted to save so she had money for me and Ben for clothes, birthdays, or Christmas. One night they were about to start their cleaning as Patricia placed a wide hairband over her perfectly asymmetrical blonde jaw length hair. She was chatting away to her younger sister when she realised, she obviously wasn't listening.

"What's wrong? You're miles away tonight."

"Derek saw the post office savings book and went mad. He's closed the account. He said all my wages should go towards the food shopping." Patricia was furious but not surprised. She remembered a time, during a family party when her husband Francois was chatting to Derek and was left speechless by his brother-in-law's attitude. Patricia recollected,

"I told him how you deal with all our finances because you are better at it" Francois had told her. "He said surely you don't show her your pay packet?" he continued "He then said you should never let your wife know what you earn." Francois told Derek that yes, he did, as it should be in a marriage. He then made his excuses and walked away incredulous. So, Patricia was not surprised by the post office account saga, but she was furious with Derek and worried for her sister.

"Why don't you leave him Bern? You know mom and dad would look after you, Ben and Lauren." Bernadette's reply was almost a whisper,

"But I love him" and Patricia felt like banging her head against the wall. There had never been any love lost between Patricia and Derek. She didn't like the way he spoke to her sister from the very first moment she met him. He thought Patricia was a busy body because she spoke up for herself and her sister.

Shortly after this, when I was two, mom asked dad for some money to get her hair cut, dad said no. She was sick of it, sick of never having a penny to her name, sick of him and now simply sick as something inside her snapped. Her fists and teeth clenched, and she started to rock to and fro on the chair. After hours passed and his wife had not moved or uttered a word, Derek finally took notice. Her fists and teeth still clenched, still rocking, unresponsive to anything he said as she fixed her stare at some faraway place.

Later that evening he drove us all to Lucy and Henry's because he didn't know what to do with their daughter. She sat on her parents' sofa, still clenched, still rocking, still speechless. After six years of marriage, she had suffered a nervous breakdown, diagnosed by psychiatric doctors at Highcroft Hospital, where she would be sectioned for the next twelve months. Her depression was so severe that the usual treatment did not work. Doctors resorted to electric shock treatment. She told Patricia that she was strapped to a table and given something to bite down on. Afterwards her teeth were loose. It was known to cause loss of emotional responses and apathy, which it did, dampening her true personality and spirit.

Dad decided that I should stay with his brother's family while Ben stayed with his sister's family. Obviously, I don't remember it but I know I was loved and looked after very well. Ben however was six and overnight had gone from an undisciplined home life to a very strict one in comparison, away from his mom, dad, and sister. He was loved and looked after just like me, but he was removed from everything he had ever known. He was so unhappy he returned home to dad after just a few months. I was with my auntie's family for almost a year. Ben and I were never close growing up and I'm certain this early separation paved the way for that. Nan Lucy and Grandad Henry had offered to look after us both, keeping us together, on the understanding that we went home to dad at weekends. Instead, dad turned to his own family, not foreseeing the damage that would be caused by separating his son and daughter. Luckily for me, for reasons I do not understand, babies tend not to retain memories. I'm sure it must have affected me too, but the oblivion of my formative years enveloped me like a comfort blanket.

Lauren Love

Little Boxes 1974

On the day of mom's discharge, in early 1974, dad took her to their first mortgaged house on a new council estate on the outskirts of Birmingham. Ben and I were six and two. I wonder if a new home was a comfort to her or unsettling at that point. Either way it was a new start, and we were all back together.

Our house was identical to all the others on that side of our road, a three-bed semi with a garage and a drive for dad's car. Little boxes, all the same, except for the lives that played out inside them. I was never far from mom's apron strings, enjoying so much pre-school time just the two of us, while Ben was at school and dad was at work. Mom would usually be found sat in one of the faux leather, brown armchairs, her legs folded under her, sitting to one side. I would usually be found squeezed into the space between her legs and hip. She never once complained that I was squashing her, nor did she ever suggest I sit anywhere else on the rest of the empty three-piece suite.

One day while mom was in a deep sleep in that chair, I as a toddler gently placed my thumb under one of her eyes and my forefinger on her eyelid, separating them to open her eye.

"Talk a me mommy, talk a me." She opened her so tired eyes, smiled her mommy smile and made herself sit up to stay awake. A few years later I would worry less than my toddler self as I would understand by then it was a side effect of her medication. She was the best mom of all the moms, of all the little boxes, my friends often enviously said so, but she was, as my reception teacher would say, 'a sleepy sausage.' Ben and I squabbled, as siblings do, and dad always seemed to bring a dark cloud with him. It often felt like he didn't notice we were there, turning the TV on as soon as he came in, drowning out the music mom was listening to. He would lie on the settee in his black, oily clothes from working at his car body repair garage. Hours could go by without him uttering a word to any of us. Where we grew up, the three meals of the day were, breakfast, dinner, and tea. So there dad would lie until mom handed him his tea.

Someone once said, the best thing a man can do, as a father, is show his children how much he loves their mother. That's all I ever wanted from dad. Not once did I see mom and dad hold hands, kiss, hug, hold a conversation even. Never a shared glance, never a sense that they were a team, like nan Lucy and Grandad Henry. I knew they had a physical relationship; walls were thin in our little box. But to me it seemed in such stark contrast to everything I witnessed, that I could not reconcile it in my logical head. One thing I knew, from a very early age ... marriage was not for me.

I Thought We Had Years

The Promise 1976

My nan Lucy gently coaxed me into being less fidgety, while combing my blonde hair into pig tails. "Keep still bab, I'm nearly done. We've got to have your hair looking lovely for your mom, haven't we." Mom was poorly again, and we were going to see her. I just wanted to get there, to see mom, not caring about the state of my hair. But I loved my nan and grandad, I felt safe with them. Grandad Henry would have driven us, though I don't remember the journey. The destination would have been Highcroft Psychiatric Hospital, though I don't remember arriving there. I was transported from having my hair combed in nan's kitchen to standing by mom's bedside.

I was five and trying to be so brave, but I was scared because she was so still, so different. Her shiny, thick brunette hair was dull and messy, why had nobody made her hair nice? Her arms that used to hold me were so thin. I felt my bottom lip start to tremble as she looked towards me but as if she couldn't see me. That moment was so painful, then it melted away as she smiled, no words, but a smile like no other. A smile that promised me, no matter how low the manic depression took her, she would always come back to me, always.

Lauren Love

Ugly People 1977

Dad had driven us to Western Super Mare, the near-est seaside resort, towing the dandy he had just bought. I hated it. It was a trailer which folded out either side into two double beds, which pushed back into sofas during the day, with a narrow walkway in between and a sink and cooker at the end of the walkway between the heads of the beds. When your six years old, sharing a bed with your ten-year-old brother who you constantly squabble with is not much fun. Dad would attach an awning for extra space. He paid us all more attention when we were on holiday.

Standing in the holiday park chip shop queue, I was holding mom's hand. Dad and Ben were going to meet us back at the dandy. What made the woman next to mom act so nasty? Was mom taking too long to order? Had she not got enough money? Had she bumped into her? I have no idea. You miss a lot when you are only as tall as the adults' waistlines. But what you never fail to pick up on as a little person is whether people are ugly or beautiful. I don't mean their faces, I'm not tall enough to care about that, I mean who they are. Maybe ugly people stood out like sore thumbs to me because I spent most of my time with such a beautiful one.

This ugly person pushed mom and said something to her in an ugly tone, mom gripped my hand tighter and looked embarrassed. I felt pure rage, waited until the ugly woman was distracted and stomped as hard as I could on her foot. She looked around sharply. As she looked down at me unsuspecting of a sweet little girl with blonde pig tails, I piped up,

"Don't you talk to my mom like that." Mom stifled a proud giggle as she turned on her heels clutching our fish and chips in one hand and squeezing my fingers tight with the other.

Lauren Love

The Sleepover 1979

I was now eight and had never had a night away from home. I rushed back from school every day, running as fast as I could to get home while all the other kids sauntered along. Once home I never ventured further than the back garden. Though mom would encourage me to go out and play in the drive that ran behind the back of the houses, I never did until I was about ten.

It's strange that I was aware of my unusual need to be near mom. Aware that it was unusual I mean. But I never let it worry me at all and I never questioned it. This need would never leave me throughout my life. I felt like she was my 'reason to be' to protect her, to love her.

My best friends were Ellen who lived two streets away and Libby from two doors down. They both came to our house all the time. Ellen appealed to my free spirit, especially once I discovered there was a world beyond our back garden and school. We were always out playing, walking, or climbing trees.

Libby was a different kettle of fish altogether; she would love nothing better than to come to our house and play endlessly with my dolls house, which bored me to tears. On many such occasions I would leave her to it while I went to play kickabout football with Marty next door. I was a tomboy with short blonde hair and never out of my jeans, torn at the knees from scuffs and scrapes rather than a point of fashion. When I got back home mom would roll her eyes and laugh at the muddied state of me. She would nod over towards Libby who was still engrossed in her make-believe dolls house world, not showing any sign of having missed me at all. Libby's parents asked if I would like to have a sleepover at their house. Surprisingly I said yes without a thought, but wished I hadn't, come that night.

Sleep would not come. I felt too misplaced. Libby's house had fallen into darkness hours since. My first and last sleepover, willing the sun to rise so I could get back to mom, next door but one. I felt trapped, the inability to get home causing panic to rise in me. The way I felt during that long, night, was to be the theme running through a recurring dream my whole life: Waking, exhausted, panic stricken and heartbroken that no matter how I tried, I could not get back to her.

Lauren Love

The Unmissed Pennies 1982

I didn't know at the time that it wasn't the norm. Dad would regularly come home from the pub with a takeaway just for himself, sitting in front of the TV without asking if we wanted any. One such night, as he was well into his Kentucky fried bucket meal, it seemed to suddenly dawn on him that he had a family in the same room. He asked if we wanted any. We declined, feeling like we were being fed scraps.

Every night he lay on the settee. He would not hear his loose change tumbling out of his jean pockets, over the noise of the television. Each day while he was at work, mom would make it a joint mission to see how much we could find wedged between the cushions. Sometimes we found a few pounds worth, and mom would give me a hug saying,

"Chinese this Friday." Whatever the retrieved amount, we would count it up and she would always give me some for sweets. Come Friday evening, we would take the twenty-minute walk up to the shopping precinct. Our pace picked up as we walked under the underpass   , keeping an eye over our shoulder. Once out the other side our eyes were set on the Chinese takeaway in the far corner of the L shape of shops. There were usually young lads in groups hanging around, so mom kept a tight hold of my hand and her bag. We would order a chicken fried rice to share and if we were flush a banana fritter. Whenever Ben was home, she would order his favourite too. If any pennies were retrieved over the weekend, we had a midweek treat night too when the sweetie van came down our street.

"Come on Lauren, see what you fancy" Mom would say excitedly. We would have a quarter of midget gems, blackcurrant liquorice, chocolate raisons or rum truffles between us. It was ten minutes of excitement as we queued outside the van, chatting to our neighbours. Once we were armed with our quarters of sweets, we headed back to mom's chair and curled up in front of the television having a sugary feast. When we were together, I felt like we had a rosy glow around us. It wasn't lost on me though, that the money dad never even missed, was money that made all the difference in the world to mom. Pennies with which she would treat her children, the way she always wanted to.

Lauren Love

Dinner is Served 1983

I was now twelve, Ben sixteen and rarely home, mom and dad thirty-five. My paternal nan, Lilian had remarried a man called Fred. I loved Fred, he made me laugh. I was the child he never had. To me he was a father figure minus the dark cloud. I often spent weekends with them at their house, sometimes my friend Irene would come too. For the life of me I cannot remember how often I went there. Surely not every weekend? This was a strange hiatus where I never gave a second thought to mom who I was leaving on her own to all intents and purposes.   Nan and Fred would pick me up on Friday evening or Saturday morning, take me to the Dog Racing Stadium where mom and Patricia worked on the Saturday night and bring me home on Sunday. Mom knew Fred was a good man and thought the world of me. I suppose for me and Irene, weekends there made us aware of the less than harmonious atmosphere in our own homes. As that became clearer, we awaited our weekends away more and more eagerly. During the week, there was school of course which I absorbed myself in, still rushing back home when the bell rang to spend time with mom. Our routine stayed the same.

But one night, for some reason mom decided that routine would change. Dad came home as normal, switched the TV on as normal, lay on the sofa as normal, never spoke as normal. Mom got out of her armchair as normal, warmed his tea up as normal and decided she would not be serving it as normal. She walked the few steps from the kitchen to the living room and without a sound, she held his full dinner plate aloft and turned it upside down on his head. I don't know if he had done something to rile her, or if the day in day out, of him had finally got to her. We both ran into the kitchen, pulling the door shut, just dodging the empty plate he had thrown at it. The dent in that door was still there when our little box was repossessed about ten years later.

Goody Two Shoes 1984

Mom was trying to tempt me to bunk off school as she said mischievously, "Stay home today, we can have some fun, go on." I can count on one hand how many mornings she would have been up while I was getting ready to go to school and on each of those occasions this is exactly the sort of thing she would say with a glint in her eye. I do not know what possessed me to go to school that day and all the others. It was a trait I would find hard to shrug off in later life. Feeling more comfortable to keep going on automatic pilot than to dare to stop for a moment and step off the treadmill I was on. Such a bloody goody two shoes. Denying myself precious time with the person who would teach me the real lessons in life.

I Thought We Had Years

Lauren Love

Choose Life 1984

Looking down onto the right-hand side of the stage at Birmingham NEC, me and my schoolfriend Irene had rushed out of our Seats. Like all the thousands of other thirteen-year-old Wham fans, we wanted to get as close to the stage as possible, ready for the best possible view of George Michael and Andrew Ridgely's when they appeared.

Mom had been saving a long time for these tickets. I secretly loved listening to her favourite singer, Barry Manilow, with her at home. She was relieved when my allegiance to Duran Duran fell by the wayside as Wham became my main reason for watching Top of the Pops. Only then did she admit she thought Duran Duran were 'a bit of a bloody row.'

I was so excited; I had never been to a concert before. As I turned to look for mom, I couldn't help but smile at her, totally laid back amidst the hysteria. There she sat in a sea of empty chairs, crossed legged, tapping her foot to the music, a cigarette between her fingers, beaming at me. The volume of the crowd increased so I turned around to see George and Andrew bounce onto the stage in their bright white 'Choose Life' T- shirts. It fleetingly flashed into my mind that mom was more akin to Wham than Barry Manilow. Despite everything, she always chose life and made it more colourful while she was at it. I'm pretty sure I saw George double take as he looked past us to the only person in the entire arena who was still in their seat and I'm certain I saw him smile at her.

Lauren Love

Manic Mischief 1986

D ad was in bed, his snoring telling us the coast was clear. It was either the weekend or the school holidays as it was way past midnight, and I was still up. Mom was full of energy, being a night owl naturally and probably edging towards the manic side of her condition.

The old-fashioned dark wood radiogram had taken up a five foot by two-foot chunk of our living room floor space for the past seven years. It was my paternal grandad's and when he passed away, dad decided this was his keepsake. Although it looked ridiculous in our house, it was well used. Over and over, I would play the Soundtrack to Grease LP, the Abba 'Arrival' LP I won in a fancy dress competition as a Punk (thanks to mom's imagination and one of dad's old shirts) and of course, Duran Duran and Wham. Ben played his records on there, mostly soul music. I thought it sounded really sophisticated but he wouldn't let anybody else touch them. Mom used it by far the most playing her collection of singles from the sixties. I loved them, 'Hats off to

Larry' by Del Shannon, 'Hey Jude' by The Beatles, 'Take Good Care of my Baby' by Bobby Vee. I hardly ever remember dad using it.

"Let's rearrange the furniture" mom suggested with a mischievous glint in her eye. I was always moving my bedroom around, so I was more than happy to assist. We moved chairs, settee, radiogram this way and that, never able to make it all fit.

"The radiogram has to go" said mom, like it could be magicked away. How we manoeuvred it, stifling our giggles, trying not to wake dad, was nothing short of magic. Through the lounge door, up a few stairs, swinging it around into the three-foot space between the foot of the stairs and front door. Then slowly pulling up the garage door to soften its creaks, completing the final leg of the journey to its new home, adjoined to us but separate and out of sight. We came back in and both of us flopped into mom's chair giggling as quietly as we could, looking around proudly at our new spacious living room.

I don't recall the inevitable fallout from that night as dad would not have been happy with our antics, but the radiogram found its way back into the living room and every record we played on it from then produced a shared mischievous grin between me and mom.

Lauren Love

Whelks and a Cheeky Flutter 1987

Hall Green Dog Racing Stadium was almost like a second home to me and a saviour to Mom. Here, she was Bernadette, seen, heard, and loved. She had worked on the Tote selling betting tickets on a Wednesday, Friday, and Saturday night, for the past thirteen years. It was her lifeline after the breakdown.

Patricia worked alongside her. I joined the team of glass collectors when I reached fifteen. Nan Lilian and Fred met there, well actually me and Fred met there, and I introduced him to Nan. He made her the happiest I ever saw her. Nan Lucy tried to introduce me to barley wine on a night out here, I can still taste it, she was a braver woman than me, drinking that stuff!

Tonight, I was with nan Lilian. I always knew in an instant if I liked someone by the way they were with mom. I liked all her colleagues in the booth, Patricia, Celia, Ruth, Sylvia, Beryl and of course Patricia. I hung back waiting for mom to serve the last person in her queue, giving her just enough time to place a cheeky flutter on the race before the start bell went off. Those cheeky flutters would lose them their beloved job if their boss found out. The race start bell was preceded by fifteen distinct notes ringing out of the speakers, a non-tune, but one I would always remember.

"You ok?" she asked huddling in towards the window hatch, reaching out to hold my hand, with that big mom smile.

"Yes, I'm fine. Nan said she's not having numbers two and four anymore as those dogs must be getting tired by now" I told her, both of us rolling our eyes and chuckling.

"Hello Lauren, dear"

"Hello Lauren"

"Ooh its Bernie's daughter" came all the voices from the booth, tumbling over each other and a loving finger-fluttering wave from Patricia at the back. We could hear the race building up to the finish line. The punters voices were escalating, carried by the cheering, and jeering en masse, not long left to chat. Mom put her hand into her pocket and passed me two fifty pence pieces.

"Would you get me some whelks and you have what you like"

"Well, it won't be whelks" I said pulling a 'don't know how you eat those' face, "Thanks mom" and off I went. The seafood stall was only there on a Saturday night, whelks for mom, cockles for me, drowned in vinegar, we loved it, a real treat. It was over the other side of the track, but I knew this place like the back of my hand, weaving in and out of the crowds and getting back to mom's window before the race had finished. Mom quickly popped a whelk into her mouth, hoping she could finish the marathon chewathon it took to eat one before her next customer. I had just turned to walk away when I heard a kerfuffle. As I turned around, I saw Patricia, Beryl, Celia, Ruth, and Sylvia all closed in around mom's window. They were behind her, alongside her, to her left and right, all glaring at the man at the window. Apparently, he had taken offence to mom's eating whilst serving him and had told her so in his ugly tone. He was told sternly by Patricia that his attitude would not be tolerated at this booth and to place his bets elsewhere. Mom was sat in her protective huddle, determinedly finishing her whelk.

The following Saturday, Patricia rang to tell mom she couldn't drive her to the dogs tonight, as she was full of a cold and going to stay home. Dad came in from work, mom asked him for the bus fare to get the three buses to the dog track. It never occurred to me how odd it was that she didn't ask him for a lift, we both knew there was no point asking. But It did surprise us both when he refused her the bus fare. In all the years she worked there, the £40 housekeeping dad gave her each week reduced to £19, telling her to use her £21 wages on the food shopping. There was never any leftover for bus fares, mom walked everywhere, even when dad's car was sat on the drive. That night, mom stayed home, dad went to the pub to spend multiple bus fares on beer and I, from that day, slowly saved for driving lessons.

I Thought We Had Years

Lauren Love

All Dressed Up and Nowhere to Go
1987

O kay so mom was edging towards mania, but only edging, bubblier than normal. It was New Year's Eve and for once she wanted dad to take her out, nowhere special, just wherever he was going. Dad wasn't home yet.

"I'm going to dress up really nice, so your dad wants to take me out, come and help me choose what to wear Lauren" she said with the excitement of a teenager preparing for a first date. Her excitement was infectious, and I just did not see what was coming.

Mom quickly decided herself what she was going to wear: a black fifties style dress, just above the knee, a black silken shift covered in black tassels, a black matching necklet. It had been in her wardrobe for years, but I had never seen her in it.

"You look amazing mom, so classy", she always dressed fabulously as a teenager, I had 'wowed' at many of the photos in our albums. This was the first time I had seen her dressed up for real. She looked happy with her choice, a little nervously excited perhaps, but happy. Dad came home soon after and the happiness abruptly ended when he refused to take mom out with him. I don't remember what he said to her, but she visibly shrunk into herself. I erupted with anger, how could he dismiss her like that, she was his wife, it was New Year's Eve, she looked beautiful, he should have been proud to be out with her. Through my red mist, I did not notice mom walk slowly out of the living room and upstairs to get changed back into the clothes she had on before. Meanwhile I was ranting at a man I was ashamed to call dad, stunned by his coldness. Most sixteen-year-olds who dared to speak to their dad like this, would have been told off, 'who do you think you are talking to' would have been the expected response. Instead, he fixed his disinterested gaze away from me and muttered,

"Rubbish, you don't understand"

"So, explain it to me." I pleaded. He did not utter another word. Mom came downstairs. Dad went up, got changed and went out. Mom sat in the armchair with her legs tucked behind her. I squeezed into my usual spot between her hip and legs, hugging her while she sobbed for hours, past midnight and into the New Year.

Lauren Love

The Devil is in the Detail 1988

Mom's decline from then was rapid, not sleeping or eating, not wanting to go up to bed, just sitting in her armchair, her stare fixed on some faraway place. One night, when dad came in late from the pub, I asked him to sit with her and to not leave her, while I go up and get a few hours' sleep. My gut told me it was a bad move, that I could not trust him to look after her, but my tiredness took over. I woke suddenly, bolt upright as dawn broke, knowing I had done the wrong thing. All I could hear were dad's snores from the bedroom next to mine. I rushed downstairs.

Strange how the first thing that hit me was not her now completely catatonic state, nor was it the pool of blood she was sat in (suffering from heavy periods), rocking forwards and backwards with fists clenched. What stopped me in my tracks was that she was sat on the edge of the settee, not tucked up in her armchair as I left her. She never sat on the settee, only dad did.

I phoned Patricia, I was useless, she was with us in no time and brilliant, taking mom upstairs to sort her out in the bathroom. I sat downstairs, stunned by how broken Mom was, how practical Patricia was. Searching for a reason, a black cloud smothering my heart as the snores from upstairs became louder and louder in my head.

Lauren Love

Magical Moment on a Psychiatric Ward 1988

L ater that day, a psychiatric doctor and nurse came to the house. They said mom would not get better unless she was sectioned and taken to Highcroft Hospital in Erdington, a twenty-minute drive away. Mom looked questioningly at Patricia as she reassured her, they would make her better, that we would follow on in the car with her things. She then turned to dad and looked through him. My heart was ripped from my chest as she then fixed her gaze on me, her eyes pleading, her mouth trying to smile. She had been through this before and knew the long painful journey that lay ahead, knowing her husband would give consent for several courses of shock treatment over the following months, guided by the doctors. She would have no say, no voice, as it had been all her married life.

I Thought We Had Years

"It's as if I'm in a cocoon, no-one can get in and I can't get out. It's so lonely in here. B"

Patricia would drive me to see mom in her car every Sunday teatime. I would go up three times in the week on the buses. Ben had set up home with his girlfriend Dawn and two-year-old son Jack, two years previous. So, with mom in hospital and my anger towards dad confounding with his lack of visits, I was rarely at home.

For many months, mom's recovery was so slow it was barely noticeable. She rarely spoke. She looked so frail, so tired and so scared. She wasn't eating, sleeping, or washing. But one day as I sat beside her on the edge of her bed, holding her hand in mine, I felt her start to relax. She let me wash her hair and then we sat in the communal lounge. It was sparse and the furniture was very basic. The sofas and chairs were upholstered with hard wearing dark red vinyl with wooden arms and legs. It always struck me that there were no cushions. Everything had hard lines with nothing to soften them. The pictures on the walls were those painted by the patients during occupational therapy sessions. At first glance they looked like cheerful pictures that you might find on the walls of a primary school. But the more time I spent there, I realised anguish, frustration, and sadness screamed out from those walls. I hated that mom was in there, I worried if she was safe as some of the patients could be aggressive. The nurses seemed lovely and while I was in awe of them and thankful to them, I always wondered if any of them could be mistreating mom, how would I know? You often heard of these horror stories on the news. I felt helpless.

There were plenty of patients wandering in and out of the lounge that day in varying states of agitation and distress. But it was as if we were the only two people there, as mom lay down on her side on the sofa with her head in my lap. As she fell asleep for the first time in days, I stroked her hair, unable to take my eyes off her lovely peaceful face. Finally, the battering storm inside her head had calmed, if only for a little while.

"Manic Depression
This illness is like an invisible worm, it's in your head and it gnaws at your brain and mixes up all your thoughts, it drains you to the depths. B"

I Thought We Had Years

Lauren Love

First Interview 1989

Mom returned home and was gradually feeling stronger over the last year. I was doing my A-Levels at a Sixth Form College just a forty-five-minute walk from home. I had no idea what I wanted to do workwise. All I knew was I didn't want to go to university for the sake of it. If I was going to continue studying, I wanted it to be leading somewhere, qualifying me for a particular job, but I had no idea what job. I went to my careers interview with the school where I was asked what subjects I was best at.

"P.E. and Maths" I said without hesitation. P.E. was completely glossed over as the careers advisor said,

"You would be best suited to a career in accountancy or quantity surveying"

"What's quantity surveying?" I asked her

"Quantity surveyors are the accountants of the construction industry" came the boring answer. I thanked her and walked out, wishing maths wasn't my best subject. I started applying for jobs and mom took me shopping for an interview outfit. She bought me a beige smart shirt dress with a belt and smart court shoes with a small heel. I chose them, I liked shirt dresses, they were me and I thought to get the right job it was important that I presented myself in something I was comfortable in. Obviously, mom thought I looked beautiful and anyone who didn't give me a job was an idiot.

I went for an interview with a firm of accountants in Birmingham city centre. I sat in the glass walled waiting room looking out at the vast open plan office. My nerves subsided as I looked out at row upon row of an equal mix of men and women looking almost robotic, crunching numbers, I guess. I suddenly pictured myself amongst them and did no more than stand up, tell the receptionist this job was not for me and left.

Shortly after I had an interview at a Quantity Surveyor's office in Edgbaston. I had read the job description and to my own surprise I quite fancied it. The fact that I actually wanted the job, meant I was much more nervous this time, which mom, with her extra sensory mom perception, picked up on. So, she suggested we have a day out together in Birmingham city centre after my interview, she said she used to work in Edgbaston, so she knew where I needed to go and would come along if I wanted her to – I did. The job was to be four days per week in the office paid work and one day per week at university studying a part-time quantity surveying degree at Wolverhampton Polytechnic.

On the bus ride into the city centre, as we sat up front on the top deck, I asked mom what jobs she had. She told me she started work at seventeen at Birmingham University in an office, but she left because she wasn't using the skills she'd learnt at college. She then went to work for a PR Consultant in Edgbaston, a job she really liked, and she stayed there until she got married when she was nineteen. I saw a glimpse of something in her eyes I had never seen before, a glimpse of the life she left behind I suppose. The future she could have had. I said what a shame it was that she had to give her job up to have a baby and get married. She turned to me and said,

"Oh, but if I hadn't, I wouldn't have you."

By the time we got off the bus in Edgbaston it was raining heavily. Mom spotted the road we were looking for, directly off the main busy Hagley Road. It was about quarter of a mile long and tree lined, drawing us down towards the building where my interview was to be held. The building captured my imagination straight away. It looked steeped in history, with its dark brickwork encasing two floors over an irregular shaped footprint. It was not uniform but seemed to go off in different directions, changing constantly, as we approached it. Mom had intended to wait outside but we both went inside to shelter from the rain. The receptionist greeted us with a heartfelt smile when I told her I was here for my interview, but could my mom wait here in reception for me. It was my first interview for a proper job, only having done weekend or evening part time work before while I was at school. I stepped into the office where three middle aged men sat behind a desk, welcoming me in and offering me a seat. Their questions were bazaar, asking me how I would get across a river if I was with two other colleagues and had nothing other than a plank of wood. I answered the question logically, thinking this is going to be a funny job. But bottom line was they seemed like nice people, they had a warmth to them somehow, no ugly people vibes here. I had no idea what they made of me, whether I had answered any of the questions correctly or if I could do the job. I walked back into the reception area where mom sat looking far more nervous than me. We walked out of the front door thanking the receptionist as mom linked my arm asking me how it went. The receptionist shot us the same smile as she had when we entered, like we had reminded her of something close to her own heart. Once outside, mom told me she had been telling her how clever I was and how proud she was of me. I don't know if it was down to me or mom or if it was a joint effort, but I was offered the job a few weeks later. And even when my A-Level results fell short of the mark, they still wanted to take me on. My study day was to be spent on a two-year HNC Building Studies placement and after that I could continue onto the quantity surveying degree at university.

I loved that job, I got to play with numbers which came easy to me. I got to go on site at least once per week and with my first month's wage I bought myself a wax jacket and boots for the building site visits, to go with the glamourous hard hat that was always thrust at me. I was the only female in the office apart from Audrey who was the comptometer operator. She looked after us all like a mother hen. They all took me under their wing and looked out for me as the baby of the office.

Mom loved hearing all my stories about work. How, when I went missing on site, whichever of the chaps from our office I was there with, always knew they would find me up in the roof space, the higher up I could get the better. How Jeff would bring me in plums from his tree. How Des would clear his desk like a surgeon preparing his operating table, to lay out his same lunch every dinnertime including salt and pepper pot. How Audrey made us tea and toast at eleven o'clock every morning and one day she bought a bag of sweets in the shape of fried eggs and put one on each of our pieces of toast. Now I was earning a wage I found, like mom at my age, I loved nice clothes and had some fabulous smart outfits for the office. Mom loved seeing me in them, her favourite was a mustard knee length playsuit with white polka dots.

"My beautiful, clever girl" she would say, beaming.

I Thought We Had Years

Lauren Love

A Cap, A Gown and One Very Proud Mom 1991

The last two years had been full on, four days per week getting two buses to work in Edgbaston, one day per week getting two buses to college and weekends spent largely studying. I had a boyfriend, Phillip who was more of a friend to me, but things were becoming awkward as he was more serious about our relationship than I was. It's obvious to me now that he was a comforting distraction from all the times when mom had been poorly. Now I had work and studying, I was going through the motions with him really which wasn't fair on either of us.

I had passed my HNC and there was a presentation ceremony to be held at Wolverhampton University. Mom couldn't wait, we made a day of it. The 'fast' bus which took an hour and a half, got us there much too early so we headed to McDonalds for a breakfast. The presentation was no big thing to me, I was only doing the HNC because I had done so badly in my A-Levels, I should have been two years into my degree by now. But being out with mom made such a lovely change and so it became a special day.

When we got there, they passed me a cap and gown. I told them I was not a degree student and they pointed out the different colours on the cap and gown were for HNC students or Degree students. Well mom's face lit up, and when I went up on stage to collect my certificate, all I could see was her proud beaming smile amidst all the other parents. My friend Claire who I had met on the course was there too and mom was sat next to Claire's mom. Most other students had both parents there, so it was nice that they had paired up and were having a good chat. These were not the days of mobile phones and neither me nor mom had a camera, so the official photographer's photo was purchased eagerly by mom with a few copies for family. It held pride of place on top of the fireplace surround at home. I so wish I had a photo of the two of us that day. To have captured mom's pride would have been a much better photo.

Empty Nest & Birthday Banners 1992

A few things had happened in the last year. My works office had relocated to Bromsgrove which meant a two and a half hour commute each way. I had started driving lessons but was spending more and more time at Phillip's parents' house because it reduced my commute by forty-five minutes, very bad reason, I know. Obviously, I still saw mom, but I was always coming or going, no quality time. So caught up in my busy life I never stopped to think the effect this would have on her. When I was twenty, I passed my driving test, my second attempt. I pulled up outside our house and mom came out desperate to know how I'd done. My instructor winked at me, got out of the car, walked up to mom, and pretended I had failed. As I'm a terrible liar even before opening my mouth mom looked at me and said,

"You fibbers, you've passed haven't you" then gave me a huge hug. Grandad Henry was buying a new car so, he sold me his red Volkswagen Polo for £1,000 which was a bargain. I took out a bank loan and enjoyed the forty-five-minute drive to and from work each day, making life much easier.

Today was my twenty first birthday. When I arrived at work, my desk had banners and balloons strewn across it, and I was spoilt rotten with a homemade cake that one of the chap's moms had made and so many gifts. I was so touched; it was a fabulous day and I got to go out on site and wear my hard hat gear to top it all off. When I got home mom had put a birthday banner across the top of the lounge window and balloons. I couldn't believe it; mom could barely afford to have bought them and it would have been a big thing for her to have put them up on her own. I walked towards the front door with a tear in my eye, already feeling guilty that I would be rushing in and back out.

As I walked out of the house barely an hour later, that was the first moment since I left school, that I realised she had an empty nest and I kept leaving to gate-crash somebody else's nest, which increasingly felt wrong. I felt in limbo. Mom must have been lonesome.

Lauren Love

The Repossession 1993

I was now twenty-two and had been made redundant from work. The writing was on the wall after the relocation and redundancies were inevitable. I was one of many. My trainee engineer friend Brenda who lived by me was unlucky too. As we were neither school leavers, nor fully qualified, trying to find work in our chosen fields was proving impossible. We signed on together at the local jobcentre for a very long six weeks, by which time we made a pact to get a job, any job. Anything would be better than going there each week. I got a job as a cashier at a petrol station and Brenda got a job in a biscuit factory. In the meantime, I had lost my cherished Volkswagen polo and was still paying off the loan. A drunk driver had gone into the back driver's side of me while I was stopped at a zebra crossing. Dad took the car to his garage and told me it was a 'write off'. I found out from Ben years later that he had fixed it up and sold it on. Strangely this did not surprise or bother me. Dad was clearly struggling financially. He had asked me if I would take the mortgage on in my name, but he would continue the payments. I said that if I did that, I would not be able to get a mortgage of my own until it was paid off, dad said he understood. But my real concern was if dad fell behind on the mortgage payments, it would be me with debt against my name. I often wonder should I have said yes and how differently the future would have panned out.

Shortly after, I moved into my first house with Phillip, his aunty was selling it to downsize and was leaving all her furniture and furnishings. It was a great opportunity, so we got a mortgage. There were a few unforeseen obstacles to get over; my name was blacklisted as dad had built up debt at home and any name under that same address was flagged up apparently. I suppose it was inevitable that mom would become unwell again. Ben and I had left home, and I can only imagine how increasingly isolated she must have felt living with dad while his business was failing.

Like before, me and Patricia would visit mom in hospital every Sunday together and I would get the buses there about three times per week. Mom had been in there for over six months now. I knew all the other patients, most of which had become mom's friends. They often asked mom why her husband didn't visit. Mom just shrugged her shoulders. The doctors said mom could come home for the weekend, to see how she coped with reintegrating into her life at home. She still had a long way to go, but this was the first step to returning home. She would need a lot of support.

Lauren Love

The small doctor's office contained mom, dad, me and several doctors and nurses. Mom did not utter a word. Dad began to cry. Doctors turned their attention to him, he was clearly depressed they said, but yes, she will get the support she needs, dad said. I almost combusted with anger, knowing the house was filthy, every plate and pan piled high in the sink, unopened bills forming a sizeable mound in the hallway, the house about to be repossessed. All I could bring myself to utter, desperately wanting mom home was,

"Mom is your patient, not dad, don't you think this meeting should be about her".

By the time mom was fully discharged, all that was left in the living room of her Little Box was her armchair, which had been moved to the centre of the room. She sat on the edge of her chair, no point tucking her legs up, she wouldn't be staying, she could see that. I sat on the floor. For such a small room, mom looked lost in it, looking around her, another home gone. I couldn't help but wonder if she wasn't better off in the hospital.

I Thought We Had Years

Lauren Love

A Life Lived for Others 1993

Although buying Phillip's aunt's house was a great opportunity, it was a bad decision from the outset. We were just too different and so I left, signing the house over to him. Mom and dad had moved to a council one bedroom first floor flat, and I was sleeping on the sofa whilst looking for a place to rent. Three of my friends, Irene, her sister Doris, and Ellen suggested we have a week in Ibiza. It was perfect timing for me. I phoned mom a few times from the phone box near our hotel. She'd known Ellen since I was four and Irene and Doris since I was ten. They all loved mom and always passed on their love as I headed to the phone box.

Her voice sounded different today, I knew something was wrong, but she insisted she was ok. When I returned home, she told me grandad, her quiet, gentle dad Henry had passed away on 13th April, the day before I phoned her. She hadn't told me on the phone because she didn't want to spoil my holiday. She thought the world of her dad. The path she had chosen was for him. I loved grandad Henry, but I couldn't help but wish he had been stronger for her sake. I know I would not have been born but another version of me may have. I would always have been half of her and what a life she could have had.

Lauren Love

Midnight Toasties & Classical Music
1994

I was still with mom and dad, and they had squeezed a 'put me up' bed into the lounge. As mom was tucking me in, all twenty-three years of me, she kissed me on the cheek and whispered,

"Are you hungry? I could make you a bacon and mushroom toastie"

"No thanks Mom" Mom's toasties were delicious and even more delicious somehow when eaten at midnight, making them even naughtier but nicer. But on this occasion, I declined as I was already in bed, ready for work the next day.

"Do you mind if I play a little bit of classical music before I go to bed, I won't have it on loud?"

"Of course not, it will be nice" I replied. She pressed play on her tape cassette player and sat down on the armchair only a few feet away from my bed. She perched on the edge of the chair as if she wanted to concentrate. .A lovely soothing piece of music started to play but just as it began to lull me to sleep, it reached its crescendo, passionate, heart wrenching, fabulous but most definitely not something you could sleep through. I opened one eye to see mom smiling over at me,

"Bloody good isn't it?" she said, and I couldn't help but agree as I chuckled to myself giving up any hope of getting to sleep just yet.

Lauren Love

Words Unspoken 1994

I met a man called Patrick who I fell hook, line, and sinker for. I had given mom and dad their lounge back and moved in with Ben. He and Dawn who now had a second child together Leigh, had split up, so he was renting out the two spare bedrooms. I was now managing a petrol station. A call came through for me at work.

"Lauren, I need to go to see the doctor, can you take me" I knew from her voice that it was not the GP she wanted to see. "I'll be straight there mom"

"Thank you, my guardian angel" she said so softly. The doctor immediately referred her to Solihull Psychiatric Hospital. She was not sectioned. She was not catatonic. She was asking for help before it got that bad, she knew what would come next if she didn't. She had learned the hard way so many times before. I drove her to the hospital. She stood by the window looking out from the psychiatric ward as I left to get clothes, pyjamas, and toiletries from her flat. As I turned to look back, her little face and frightened eyes broke my heart. I sobbed all the way. When I got there, I left dad a note. Driving

65

back to her, my head spinning and heart aching, asking myself the same old questions: How long had she needed me while I was too caught up in my own life to notice? How had I not seen the high before this low? My burden was always thinking I could make her better, if only I'd been there more, paid more attention, listened more, really listened to words unspoken.

Lauren Love

Locked In 1996

I can't remember how long mom was in Solihull, but not as long as normal, four months maybe. No shock treatment was needed.

Patrick had ended things with me after we had dated for six months, I was devastated. He was the one for me, so I felt really lost. He was twelve years older than me and thought I was too young for him which I think was his polite way of saying I was too clingy. I never told him but despite my promise to myself from that early age, I would have married him in a heartbeat.

During the next two years, mom would continue as always to visit her mom Lucy every Sunday afternoon with Patricia. They would take her a couple of roast dinners, change her bed, and do the housework between them. Housework was not mom's favourite pastime, but it had become their Sunday routine without thinking about it. Then they would all sit and chat together into the evening. Nan Lucy was gradually doing less herself; she was still capable but had lost the motivation since Henry passed away. She had always been so strong willed, and we all missed that version of her, our pillar of strength. Mom had started visiting her during the week as well. She would take the two-hour journey via three buses to Kings Norton, staying overnight and returning the following afternoon.

One such night towards the end of August, Lucy had more tots of brandy than she should and when it had the desired effect, it was bedtime. And if she was going to bed, her daughter was going to bed too. Mom told her she would follow her up later as she wasn't tired yet and continued watching television. She saw nan Lucy shut the door to, as she left the room and thought nothing of it, thinking perhaps it was so she wouldn't hear the television from upstairs. A little while later, heading for bed, she realised not only had she shut the door but also pulled the bolt across on the other side as she always did when she went to bed. Henry had put them on all the doors as they had been broken into before. So, mom started banging on the door and calling to her, eventually giving up but wondering how she would manage all night without access to the toilet. The next thing she heard was the doorbell ringing and all the bolts being unlocked on the front door, Lucy's voice saying,

"Oh hello" so sweetly and male voices responding to her. Mom started to bang on the door again when it opened to the sight of Lucy in her nightdress and two policemen behind her. She had thought someone was breaking in, forgot her daughter was still downstairs and called 999.

Lauren Love

The Power of Silence 1998

T he past year had been my worst so far, I had lost my way, lost sight of who I was. The split from Patrick had knocked me sideways even though I had seen it coming. I had moved out of Ben's, into my friend Doris' vacant flat. Then got together with a blatantly unsuitable man on the rebound from Patrick. More stupidly still I moved in with said unsuitable man when Doris needed to move back into her flat. Resulting in a shell of me sitting with mom, putting on a brave face, telling her about the interview I had just had for a new job.

Mom sat next to me on her two-seater sofa. This was the closest I had come to understanding the slow drip effect of withdrawing within yourself, so much so, you feel unable to ask for help even when the help you need is sitting right beside you.

"Has he hit you?" mom quietly asked. In a futile attempt to not worry her I lied

"No" She knew that she didn't need to say anything, that just listening and giving me the time to process my own thoughts, would snap me out of the fog I had become lost in. Her silence was powerful, it gave me time to realise I needed and wanted to tell her. I looked up and said, so quietly, anyone else might have missed it "Yes, he did hit me, mom" I stayed at mom and dad's flat again on the 'put me up' bed, being tucked in and fattened up on midnight toasties, both of which were exactly what I needed at that point. I was stalked daily by the ex. Both mom and dad were brilliant. Mom emotionally and dad would meet me from work when my colleague was not there to chaperone me.

In the middle of it all, after thirty-one years of marriage, when things between them had been far worse than they were now, dad left mom.

Lauren Love

Finding Her Voice 1998

D ad met me from work, as my colleague was off that day and my personal stalker would inevitably be lurking. The usual routine was for me to wave to dad in his truck, then he would wait until I got in my car and had safely driven off. But on this occasion, he got out of the truck and asked me to get inside. Nan Lilian was sitting in the middle of the three front seats. Dad told me that he had left mom, that if I was brave enough to leave my 'relationship', he could do the same. I was staggered that he could compare thirty-one years of marriage to a very brief, abusive, loveless mistake. I wanted to say this to him but all that came out was,

"It's hardly the same." Dad offered no further explanation. I got out and walked over to my car. All those years when I was growing up, believing they would both be happier if they split up. Now, as an adult, it felt surreal.

Mom told me that she heard dad and nan talking in the bedroom (mom was in the lounge), she heard them discussing their plan to move to a two bed so that nan could live with them. I should point out here that nan was fully capable both physically and mentally and was not in need of any care, but I do suspect she was lonely. Mom was furious, it was obviously a done deal, and she knew nothing about it, as always.

The most remarkable thing then happened, mom somehow found the courage to say she loved this flat and would not leave it. This may not seem remarkable but finding her voice had been a long time coming ...

"I just couldn't bring myself to stand up to you again Derek. I never challenged you after that night, never said a word when you did things I didn't like or disapproved of, but I'm over you now at last. It's taken this long to come to terms with you, 46 years, a lifetime. But I've done it and I have moved on to a better life at last. I was scared of you for years, but not anymore. I think I'm back to my old feisty self and am eventually recovering from this miserable illness, partly brought on by your mental cruelty and a mixture of circumstances. At last, I can move on and forgive and forget. At last. B"

It is not what she wanted at that point, but her husband left her to live with his mom. She had finally stood up to him and without hesitation he continued with his plan without her.

I suspect there was a financial aspect that drove dad's decision. Nan sold her share of her house, they moved to another council flat and dad held nans purse strings from that day on, as he had mom's the past thirty-two years.

Solitude 1999

Each other's company and support were exactly what me and mom needed right now. Mom was still in shock from dad's sudden departure, wondering whether she should have just gone along with him, burying her own feelings, as she always had before …

"26-6-98, It doesn't always do to say what's in your thoughts B"

It was strange, I had wished for dad to leave so many times when I was growing up. But now, was it too late for her? He was all she'd known for the past thirty-two years. She had not wanted him to go which made her strength even more remarkable to me.

So, my next move made no sense. I moved in with Patricia. Her children had all left home and she and Uncle Francois offered me one of their spare rooms. It was only a five-minute drive from mom's and the thought of my own bedroom, and a smoke free environment was too hard to resist. Mom being mom, she encouraged me to go.

"1999, Solitude, I am alone. B"

Lauren Love

A Care Home and a Recycled Cooker
1999/2000

Mom and Patricia were trying everything they could to prevent their mom going into a home, but it looked like they were out of options. Though mom's flat only had one bedroom, she tried having nan Lucy stay with her. Patricia and Francois were working full time, but they also tried over a long bank holiday weekend. Both situations were clearly untenable. Lucy had changed. It had been a slow, gradual transformation. Once the woman they looked to for love and guidance, now she was frustrated and unhappy. Her daughters could do no right by her and yet only her daughters would do. So, the two sisters were shocked and heartbroken as they went in search of a nursing home, finally settling on a place called Oakwood. It was nothing to look at, it needed a freshen up on the décor front, but it was clean, and the staff seemed competent and caring. They provided activities for all residents daily, chair exercises and singalongs. But as they suspected Lucy would not join in. She had given up long before she stepped foot in the home. It was the hardest thing Patricia and mom had ever had to do.

Afterwards Patricia would often become visibly upset. In contrast, mom's emotions were not obvious to anyone other than her sister and me. The shock treatment she had been subjected to and the side effects of her medication still caused a lack of visible emotion. As Patricia talked openly about how she'd never be able to forgive herself for putting Lucy in a home, mom stood by her side without uttering a word. The sadness in her eyes so deep they pulled me into her heavy heart.

Nan's house had to be sold to pay for the nursing home fees. Patricia and Mom kept anything of sentimental value and shared some of those things amongst us; me, Ben, and my cousins. Dad took nan's cooker, steam cleaned it and sold it back to mom for £30! In the same vein he would visit mom and mow her five-foot square piece of grass, then charge her £5 for doing it. A great hourly rate as it took five minutes. Mom paid for the cooker and the grass cutting without a second thought. It was only when the jaws dropped of anyone, she mentioned it to in passing, that she realised how mercenary her estranged husband was and always had been.

Lauren Love

Turning a Blind Eye

We were chatting about the past and I asked mom if she missed dad and why they never used to go out together. She told me of a time when me and Ben were teenagers and mom asked dad to take her to his local pub with him. She said, all night, the woman sat next to dad was rubbing her hand up and down his thigh under the table.

"Oh god, what did you do?" I asked

"Nothing"

"Didn't you say anything?" I continued

"No"

"Not even when you got home?" She shook her head

"Why not?" I persisted gently. She just shrugged.

One of mom's favourite songs was 'I Am, I Said' by Neil Diamond. The next time I heard it, I listened to the lyrics and realised why she never said anything that night.

I Thought We Had Years

…."I am"... I said
To no one there
And no one heard at all
Not even the chair
"I am"... I cried
"I am"... said I
And I am lost and I can't
Even say why

"I am"... I said
"I am"... I cried
"I am"

Lauren Love

Letting Go March 2000

om seemed to be getting stronger since dad had left. He still popped around from time to time and he sorted out any benefits she was entitled to. I believed they were rubbing along better since he had left. I don't know how I had it in me when I too left her in March 2000 to live in the Isle of Man. Patrick could not find work here after being made redundant. So caught up in my own life and impending adventure, I left.

On the morning we headed to the ferry we drove to mom to say goodbye. There were no tears, but her eyes were tired and red as if she had cried all night and all morning. She hugged me so tight and told Patrick he was to look after her little girl. She liked him and knew how much I loved him and that he was not the sort of man who would ever hurt me.

"Mom's been here, I know she has. I just know how she must have felt when she lost Dad. It was hard for all concerned but most of all for her after fifty one years of being together, never one night apart in fifty years,

79

amazing. That's True Love isn't it Lauren ....? Wish I could have known that kind of Love in my lifetime. I think you and Patrick have that kind of Love ...? B"

She knew I would be ok but my heart broke and it took everything I had to get in that car and let Patrick drive us away. The further we drove from mom, the closer we got to Heysham ferry terminal, the more I questioned what I was doing

"I don't know if I can leave her" I said to Patrick. He reassured me she would love visiting us over there but was bound to be upset today and we kept driving. But it wasn't just mom I was worried about, it was me, the further we drove, the more that panicky need to get back to her filled my heart.

"Xmas 2000, not so lonely. Still got my family and friends, though scattered to the winds. B"

Lauren Love

I'm not any mother 2001

Mom went to visit Ben and his new girlfriend at his house in Solihull. Ben hadn't visited mom for some time. Growing up he knew he couldn't help mom which killed him to the core. Mom and dad's lifestyle had always represented everything he didn't want for himself. So, selfishly he stayed away. After two buses and a bit of a walk, she arrived at his house. It was obviously a bad time because she didn't see much of him as he busied himself with other things. She ordered herself a taxi to go home and he never offered her a lift. There could have been a lot more to it, mom would never speak badly of Ben or me. But that's as much as I know. That and the fact that when the taxi dropped her off back home in the grove, dad happened to be just pulling up. He saw her burst into tears the second she got out of the taxi, sobbing as she fumbled in her pocket for her house key. It seemed that both her children had broken her heart.

I Thought We Had Years

"Nov 2001, I'm not any mother, I'm <u>his</u> mother and I should be as special to him as he is to me. But I'm not. B"

It took a while to shake the way she felt that day ...

"The rain looks like diamonds on the windowpane tonight, but they remind me that it's raining in my heart for Ben. B x"

She had an empty nest. Although I phoned her every day, I had put the Irish Sea between us. Her first born was only two bus rides away, but try as she may, she could not reach him.

Lauren Love

Surprise, Surprise 2001

I wasn't looking forward to being thirty, no idea why. So, when Patrick suggested we go to London for my birthday weekend, I thought he was just trying to cheer me up. On our first day there, we were window shopping and Patrick kept gravitating towards jewellers. I thought he must need a new watch. Then while standing in a jeweller's foyer, he stopped in front of the rings section and before I could register what he was looking at he said,

"If you weren't such a pain in the arse about getting married, I was going to buy you one of those" pointing at the engagement rings. Well, I can honestly say I did not see that coming so the only reply he got was stunned silence.

"So do you want one or not?" he asked, and, in a heartbeat, I said,

"Go on then". Don't worry, there was a follow up proposal which was made of fairy tale stuff! Apparently, Patrick had arranged a surprise get together with family, for my thirtieth birthday in Birmingham before we returned to the Isle of Man. He hadn't mentioned he was going to propose just in case I didn't say yes! He had called mom, who had phoned around everyone with the details. So, when we walked into The Swan in Coleshill, I was surprised to see them all sitting there, and they were soon equally as surprised to hear of our engagement. It was a lovely evening. Mom looked happy for us but I'm sure a big part of her was sad that her little girl was settling down so far away, but she never let on.

Lauren Love

Missing You Already April 2002

I had told mom and Patricia years ago how every time I visited nan Lucy, as I left, she would stand at the front garden gate and wave me off saying, "Miss you already." This stayed with them.

I was working the morning shift in the gym when my boss came in to tell me there was a call for me. It was mom. She never called me at work and the fact that it was during the morning shift made it odder as mom was not an early riser. I knew it was her, but her voice sounded so different.

"Lauren? "She asked, pleading for it to be me at the end of the phone after first getting my boss' voice

"Yes mom, it's me, are you ok?"

"I've got some bad news; your nan has passed away" she sounded tired and heartbroken yet reassuring at the same time. She knew how much I loved nan, and I imagined her at the other end of the phone, trying to hold back her own tears to break it to me gently. At that moment, more than ever, I think we both wished for the Irish Sea to evaporate, allowing me to just jump in the car to get to her. There were no words, but I wanted to stay on the phone, I hated the thought of her hanging up, to sit by herself having just lost her mom.

"We will come home. I will call you later to let you know when we will get there."

"Thank you, Lauren," came her gentle voice.

Apparently, mom and Patricia, had gone to the nursing home after receiving a call from one of the care staff late the night before. They arrived there around midnight and sat by her bedside until morning. Staff then advised they went home to get some rest and to come back later that day. They had only been home an hour or so, when they received another call to say nan's condition had worsened. They headed straight back over and though it was less than a half hour drive, they were too late.   Not only had they lost their mom, but they had lost her in the short time they were not by her side, they were heartbroken.

"16/4/02, Mom died, I'll never hold you again or laugh with you. Miss you already x God Bless B"

The Inscription on her headstone read, 'Missing You Already.'

Lauren Love

Self-Admission May 2002

G rief is Love that has nowhere to go and mom had nobody there to give all that love to. A little while after nan's funeral, she phoned Newington Clinic and asked to speak to Georgina. Georgina always said it was a joy to visit mom, that in all her years as a Community Psychiatric Nurse, she had never met anyone as lovely as Bernadette. Even with all her experience, she looked so saddened whenever mom reached that pivotal point of no return without hospitalisation. From mania to the deepest depression to a catatonic state, she knew the signs, not much could surprise her in that respect. Until today when she heard a courageous voice down the phone asking if she could admit herself to Solihull Psychiatric Hospital for a couple of weeks. Would she have felt the need to do that if I had lived close by? I don't know, maybe. The thing she had found most difficult in her life was,

"Spending time in mental hospitals and having shock treatment" (Journal of a Lifetime. Dear Mom, From You to Me),

and yet, here she was, going into one voluntarily, struggling to cope with the loss of her mom. She was back home a couple of weeks later but, it was the saddest, bravest thing I had ever known.

Lauren Love

A Seafront Reception 2003

T hat morning, mom helped me into my dress. It was a simple, ivory, handmade creation that I had treated myself to, thanks to mom. She had given me £500 from the money nan Lucy had left her. I could feel her hands shaking as she fastened the delicate buttons along my lower back. As I turned, we both smiled and without a word, knew what the other was thinking - that my nan, her mom was there, in that room, with us.

It was the best wedding. I'm not just saying that because it was mine, it really was. We married in the Isle of Man, in Castletown Registry Office, which was in an actual Castle. We would discover many years later, that it was one of the most sought-after wedding venues in the British Isles. Patrick had organised everything, all I had any part in, was the dress and flowers. I was nervous but excitedly so, I couldn't have been happier. Choosing to have the wedding in the Isle of Man, a place we had quickly come to think of as home, was a risk, not knowing how many of our family and friends would be able to join us. The risk paid off when most of them arrived that weekend. There were many who couldn't make it; one of my cousins, four of Patrick's nine siblings, but as he came from such a big family it felt like we still had a great turnout. Our family on the other hand, was small so when Ben did not come, his absence was the elephant in the room. Mom offered to bring Jack and Leigh who were thirteen and nine. Ben told her he didn't want his kids there if Derek was going to be there, he never called him dad.

It was only when I looked at the photos weeks later, that I noticed mom looked teary in the Registry Office, normal for the mother of the bride of course and more nervous than me. Turns out, she was nervous of dad saying the wrong thing to Patricia's family. They had never got on and things had escalated on the run up to the wedding. It had put me in two minds whether I wanted him there. I thought I was doing the right thing. I thought mom would have wanted to see me being given away by my dad, even though they were separated. I didn't realise that it was a deal breaker for Ben.

The Wedding in the Castle was a dream come true, the church blessing - the cherry on top and the wedding reception was idyllic overlooking ours and mom's favourite bay, Port Erin. It was the first-time mom had met our friends, Isobel and John, Manx born and bred, and their faces lit up as mom told them how much she loved this island. It was also strangely the first-time mom had met our friends from Birmingham, Ann and James. I was working with Ann when I moved to the Isle of Man, and we had always kept in touch. As day drifted into evening, I started to tire, so I rested next to mom and dad. Mom's hands cupped mine, she smiled at me, looking so proud and relaxed now, all nerves gone.

As the weekend celebrations came to a close, everyone headed back to the airport for their departure flights. My friend Ann gave me a big hug. As she pulled away her eyes were tearful.

"I'm going now because I can't bear to watch you and your mom say goodbye." Ann was right I couldn't bear it either. It's an unnatural feeling being somewhere that feels like the home you always wanted, but having to watch her walk away from it, from me. Now I knew how she felt.

I Thought We Had Years

Lauren Love

A Taste for Travel

Mom visited me and Patrick every year in the Isle of Man. Her first and second visit in 2000 and 2001 was with dad. They both wanted to see how we were getting on and so, although separated, they travelled over together. It was so good to see her, and it was only then that I considered how expensive it was to travel to the Island and how she must have been saving since I had left.

In 2002, she travelled alone, for the first time in her life. When I saw her face through the glass walkway of Ronaldsway Airport, I realised how difficult that had been for her. She turned and saw me at the other side of the glass, her eyes wide and searching like a child's. She pressed her hand gently against the glass and I did the same but then quickly pointed her towards baggage reclaim. I wanted to give her a hug as soon as possible.

Until suitcases began to appear on the carousel, she would not take her eyes off me. It had been a tough year for her, losing her mom, admitting herself to a psychiatric ward and now travelling alone to see me. When she finally appeared with her case, we held each other for so long, we formed an island, parting the sea of arriving passengers. She felt so tiny in my arms and as she wrapped her arms around me, I felt the pain of the last year oozing out of her.

In 2003 she travelled over for the wedding, that time travelling with Patricia and her family. In April 2004 Patricia's husband Francois passed away. From then on Patricia asked mom to go abroad with her each year and slowly there was a change in her. Despite the ongoing medication which continued to dampen her true personality, her sparkle started to shine through. To me, it was nothing short of a sprinkle of extraordinary. The thing I loved most about Patricia was that she never saw mom's illness. She only saw Bernadette, her sister, her best friend. Patricia was four when her baby sister was born, and she had loved and looked out for her every day of her life.

"You're always there, my anchor when I need you, Patricia. B"

They went to Greece, Ibiza, Rome, Barcelona, all over. For the first time in my life, I felt like mom had a life and she was finally able to enjoy it.

Lauren Love

Overnight Willpower 2003

It was a good job I was sitting down when mom called me. "I'm giving up smoking Lauren" Mom had smoked since she was sixteen and had a forty cigarettes per day habit by her twenties. Dad was on double that when he started to lose his business. Resulting in me and Ben being anti-smoking. Obviously, it was an expensive habit neither mom or dad could afford. Doctors actually encouraged mom not to quit, telling her it was good for her nerves.

"OK, what's brought this on?" I asked, still surprised by the statement and the steely determination in her voice.

"I dreamt last night that I had cancer and it's scared me, so that's it, I'm not smoking anymore." From that moment on, she never touched another cigarette.

I Thought We Had Years

Lauren Love

Better than a Sunset 2003

Our house overlooked Port Erin Bay, on the south of the island, with Milner's Tower up on Bradda Head, looking much further away than it actually was. Mom loved the Isle of Man, especially where we lived. Her favourite bay was this bay, with its sweeping sandy beach, lighthouse, and cosy nook café right next to the lighthouse. We often went there and sat outside listening to the sea. Mom loved their crab baps; Patricia loved their home-made scones. They loved everything I loved; the quaint bookshop on the corner of the lower promenade, the ice cream parlour which also did crab baps, the gift shop on the upper promenade, from which mom always bought somebody a present. Everything on our doorstep. So even if I was working, they could have a mooch about without me.

I Thought We Had Years

Today me and mom decided to take a stroll up to the bench nearest Bradda Head's summit, where we sat chatting until the sun began to set. I had told her how stunning the sunsets were here and how I often sat and watched them in the bay. But by the time we got to the bench and the sun began to set, I barely noticed it as I simply soaked up the wonder of her, sitting here right next to me.

Lauren Love

Double Egg and Chips 2004

One of the first places I ever took mom and Patricia on the Isle of Man, was to a café called Harbour Lights in the small seaside town and fishing port of Peel, highly recommended by Isobel and John. Walking in, we all instantly fell in love with everything about it: the relaxed atmosphere, the warm welcome from the waitresses, every type of teapot you could imagine hanging from the ceiling, pretty lace tablecloths, seaside memorabilia and contented chatter amongst the customers. It was busy and we sat at one of the few empty round tables along the back wall. Although all the window tables were occupied, we still had a perfect view of the beach. The reputation of this quaint café was that of very good homemade food at reasonable prices. The menu was extensive and after reading through barely half of it, I noticed a lengthy specials board on the wall too. None of us could make up our minds what to choose as it all sounded so good. Then a waitress came out carrying double egg and chips to the table next to us.

I Thought We Had Years

"That looks good," said mom. Then decisively closed her menu and forgetting all the other wonderful sounding dishes, declared, "That's what I'm having". Patricia took quite a while longer before coming to exactly the same decision. I had something different; I can't remember what. We washed it down with several cups of tea in china teacups poured from dainty teapots. We cleared our plates and mom said it was the best egg and chips she had ever had. We returned every year, me and Patricia trying something different each visit but there was no swaying mom, it was double egg and chips for her every time.

Lauren Love

Reluctant Gym Workouts 1998/2004

B efore I moved to the Isle of Man, I was regularly going to a gym in Coleshill. Mom and Patricia decided they would give it a go. They had gone to exercise classes together since I was little but never a gym. They had already had the compulsory induction so we decided what each of us would go on, it was busy, so it boiled down to what equipment was free. Mom ended up on a rower, Patricia a recumbent bike and I popped my bum on an upright bike. After five minutes Patricia had moved to an elliptical trainer. I kept looking over at mom at the other end of the gym impressed that she was on the rower for so long, even though she had slowed right down. Then she came to a stop, legs extended, hands still holding the rowing handles. I headed over to tell her how well she had done, ten minutes on the rower on her first session. She looked up at me looking decidedly unimpressed.

"I can't get out of it, I can't reach my feet." The Coleshill gym sessions soon petered out.

I Thought We Had Years

A few years after moving to the Isle of Man, I had my own fitness studio, where I taught circuit classes and Personal Training. We had bought a four-storey house and the Fitness Studio was on the ground floor. I had furnished it with reconditioned commercial cardio and resistance equipment, just like the gym in Coleshill. One rainy afternoon while mom and Patricia were staying with us, I suggested we all have a quick workout downstairs. There was a tumbleweed moment and two very unimpressed faces at such a terrible suggestion. Faces that looked at me as if to say, 'we are on our holidays you know.' Then after a long few moments mom jumped up.

"Come on then" she announced, and an amazed Patricia took her lead. After a quick change of clothes, we headed downstairs. Patricia jumped on the recumbent bike, her favourite and mom said she needed the toilet before she started, which was in the corner of the gym. Meanwhile I selected one of my class playlists from my iPod to get us going. The first track was Abba's Waterloo and just as the chorus kicked in, the toilet door flung open to reveal mom standing in classic Abba pose wiggling her hips, one arm reaching towards the ceiling, the other towards the floor belting out

"Waterloo", she wiggled over to the upright bike as me and Patricia couldn't stop laughing.

"I'm not going on that bloody rower" she adamantly.

Lauren Love

Tai Chai and Tea Dances 2005

St Annes Church Hall, adjacent to nan Lucy's funeral venue just three years ago, held a tea dance on the last Wednesday of every month. Patricia found out about it through church which she attended every week and asked mom if she fancied it. As always Patricia felt like she was railroading her into it as she persisted in getting her reluctant sister to go with her. Patricia loved it, mom grew to love it after spotting a lady walking in with various chest boxes and setting up on a table in the corner, placing various coloured nail varnishes out in front of her. Every last Wednesday in the month after that, Patricia was told not to be late picking her up as she wanted to be first in line to have her nails done.

Here they made new friends. The one I remember most was a dot of a lady called Bessy. She and mom would beam at each other, both hands holding both hands as they said how lovely it was to see each other. Bessy told her that she and quite a few of the others were going to a Tai Chai class in the neighbouring hall every Monday at ten o'clock in the morning. This pushed Patricia's

103

persuasion skills to the limit as mom was not a morning person. But the following week they were there 'Carrying the Moon' and 'Playing with Clouds' and loving it so much they went every week for the next fourteen years.

Today was the last Wednesday of the month and I was not working, so I went with mom and Patricia to this tea dance I had heard so much about. Mom introduced me to Bessy. I liked her instantly. There was a lady dressed in a fifties rock and roll baby blue skirt and cream turtleneck with a small red silken neck scarf, greeting everyone as they entered the hall. Several ladies were walking around pouring tea and coffee. Homemade cakes were plentiful on dainty plates, already laid out on the tables. As soon as we sat down, an amazing voice started belting out,

"Dooh wah diddy diddy dum diddy dooh" It was the lady in the fifties rock and roll outfit, obviously. Looking around, I could see why mom and Patricia and everyone else in the room looked forward to this. Mom spotted the nails lady setting up, so shot up out of her seat, to be first in the queue. On her way, I saw her chatting to Bessy and whatever she was saying, mom looked thrilled to bits. When she sat back down beside me, she said excitedly,

"Bessy said you are a credit to me." She couldn't have looked any happier if she had won the lottery.

Viking Festival 2006

Mom had always been fascinated by Vikings. So, when I heard that Peel was staging a Viking Festival and concert, I just had to see if she could make it. September was her preferred month to visit when all the heathers were out on the fells and the weather was cooler but still pleasant if we were lucky. This year would buck the trend. She came over with dad and though I knew it probably wasn't his thing, I ordered three tickets.

It was a three-day festival, and we went along each day. On the final day there would be a Viking burial re-enactment, that mom was eager to get a good seat for. So, we headed out an hour earlier than we had on the previous two days and were the first to choose our spot on the staggered seating. It was a beautiful open-air waiting room, on the sandy beach with the stage ready for the grand finale Abba Tribute band, set against the backdrop of Peel Castle. Seats started to fill, dad was wondering around the promenade while me and mom stayed put. About an hour before the start time, the heavens opened.

Event organisers busily passed out black bin bags for us to pop a hole in the bottom and place over our heads, as makeshift raincoats. As the rain became heavier and speculation spread about the inevitable cancellation of tonights show, the crowds quickly dwindled, making their way home. Dad was eager to do the same. Mom would not budge, she was not missing this show, come what may. By the time an announcement was made to postpone until the following evening, there was only me, mom, and half a dozen other staunch Viking fans rooted to our seats and soaked through. Dad was sheltering under a shop canopy on the promenade. Mom was happy with that outcome. We would watch the show tomorrow minus the bin bags.

The following evening, we arrived early again and waited in much better weather. It was well worth the wait, as the torch lit procession came over the hill behind Peel Castle, onto the beach, setting alight the Viking longboat and pushing it out to sea. It was a stunning spectacle, but my attention was divided between the sight before me and mom's face beside me, utterly transfixed, utterly enthralled. At the end of the re-enactment, she turned to me smiling like a Cheshire cat.

"That was fabulous" she beamed. I went to get us some drinks in the break before the Abba Tribute Band came on. We thought it would probably be decidedly average and we had seen what we had come to see but we would stay and watch the start of the concert anyway. How wrong we were, walking back to the car after midnight, dad way ahead eager to get home at long last, me and mom sauntering along, singing at the top of our voices

"Thank you for the music, the songs we're singing, thanks for all the joy they're bringing ..."

I Thought We Had Years

Love Will Change Your World Around
December 2007

B en asked Mom if he could stay with her for a little while, after selling his house, until he found a new place. Her 'Little Man' had come home. A little while turned into twelve years. I must admit, at first, I was worried that Ben would drive her mad. Though he could often make her laugh out loud, equally his moods could make her withdraw within herself again.

"you're so funny and adorable at times but like a thing possessed at others, like two people in one body. Strange, still we're all different aren't we!? B"

When I phoned her, I could tell immediately if Ben was in a good or bad mood, if it was the latter, our normal long natter about anything and everything would be diluted into a short one-sided conversation, with me doing the talking.

As time went on though, the love between mother and son, changed them both. Mom simply loved him, unconditionally, all versions of him, whether he be Dr Jekyll or Mr Hyde until Mr Hyde gradually disappeared. Ben asked her opinion on current affairs, often putting the world to rights between them as they watched the news together each evening. He made her laugh, a lot. He had allowed her to be his mom again, but more than that, he had helped her to become Bernadette again.

Only now could I see how similar they were in many ways, both stubborn, intelligent, feisty, independent, and funny.

"You're fast asleep at the moment, reminds me of the old days when you were tiny. I wouldn't put you to bed like mom said I should cos I couldn't let you out of my sight for one second. You were so precious, and I thought you couldn't be trusted to look after yourself on your own in your cot upstairs away from me. They didn't have intercoms in 1967! So, you had to stay up with me with the telly softly in the background and a soft light on. You still do that to this day. But even now you wake in a heart-beat if you hear a strange sound or maybe sense danger. I feel so safe with you here always at my side. B,"

Dad didn't come around anymore, no doubt because Ben was there. So Ben now felt he could help mom, by cleaning up the flat and putting past troubles behind them. He did a total refurbishment. Mom chose bold, modern designs in wallpaper and a new two-piece suite. Ben replaced smoke-stained carpets for stylish wood effect laminate. The biggest transformation came from knocking down hallway cupboards. This seemed to magically double the size of the flat. Mom chose a large new glass table and four high back, red and chrome chairs for this new space. So now as you ascended the stairs from the front door downstairs, you were greeted with a stylish, contemporary dining area. She rarely had visitors but when she did, she would beam with pride as they told her it was like a show home. Long gone were the years of embarrassment of not feeling able to keep up with housework and smoked stained décor.

Ben's daughter Leigh asked him every year what he wanted for Christmas, his answer year after year was 'peace of mind.' Within the next few months, he finally got his Christmas wish, simply by being with mom. Their love for each other had changed both their world's around.

"Love changes everything, how you live and how you die. Love will change your world around. B"

I Thought We Had Years

Lauren Love

We Will Always Have Paris 2008

I had planned a surprise long weekend in Paris for mom's sixtieth birthday along with Patricia. I had talked of little else for months. All my gym members were joining in my excitement and our Manx friends Isobel and John loved hearing all the details of our secret plan, knowing mom would be beside herself. I flew over from the Isle of Man to mom, telling her that we would pick Patricia up the following day and head to Birmingham Airport for a domestic flight to London. I didn't even know if there was such a flight. When we arrived at the check in desk there were no overhead signs showing destinations, just desk numbers, this was a great start. I sneakily passed a note to the check in lady letting her in on the secret and asking for her discretion. Her face started to brighten with a warm smile, then quickly straightening her face, playing along with my request.

113

Mom was happy to sit with Patricia as I checked the flight update screens, things couldn't have gone smoother. To me and Patricia, the excitement was palpable. Patricia stood up to stretch her legs, as mom bent down to look for something in her handbag.

"So where are we flying to Lauren? Charles De Gaulle?" Patricia asked casually at normal volume

"No, Gatwick" I replied startled, shaking my head, and widening my eyes at her. While mom's head was down, still searching through the contents of her bag, Patricia repeatedly banged her head against the heel of her hand, not believing her own blunder. By the time mom's head popped up, she was done with the headbanging, and I had just managed to stifle my giggles. We boarded the plane. I made sure mom and Patricia went ahead of me so that I could make a request to the air stewardess. The pilot's voice came over the tannoy just before take-off.

"I have a special message for Bernadette who thinks she is heading to London for her sixtieth birthday, but in fact Bernadette, we are flying you to Paris." Mom turned to me, still slowly absorbing the information, then quietly said,

"You little fibber." Patricia, across the aisle, was beside herself and with her hands on her heart, exclaimed,

"Oh, I think I'm going to cry."

As soon as we stepped off the plane, I pulled out my much-loved charcoal grey beret, to get into the spirit of things. Before it had reached my head, mom and Patricia decided first stop was a beret shop, they had to have one too. We wore them everywhere we went. Mom and

114

Lauren Love

Patricia's were woollen with a large black and white check, identical except for mom's had an interwoven splash of pink. They had outdone me on the beret front.

On Saturday, we headed out for a pre organised evening, starting with a river cruise along the Seine, then a three-course meal at the restaurant in the Eiffel Tower and ending the night in the theatre to watch Moulin Rouge. The latter was the highlight for mom, she loved the costumes and dancing. On other days we found our way around using the metro, visiting the Louvre, Notre Dame, sauntering along street markets, and generally packing as much into our weekend as we possibly could. On Sunday we hopped on an open top tour bus and managed to get a bird's eye view towards the front of the top deck. When it started to rain mid tour, everyone either moved downstairs or opened their umbrellas. We just kept our berets on, turned up our coat collars and giggled our way around the rest of the tour.

But the moment I will never forget was the evening at Montparnasse Tower. The lift stopped on the floor below the open-air viewing platform. We were to take a flight of stairs, which Patricia would have struggled with, suffering with her knees. So, while Patricia admired the 360-degree views of the city from the glass walled bar and restaurant, me and mom made our final ascent. We stepped out onto the large square platform and made our way over to the railing on the righthand side. I was aware that other tourists were coming and going, moving around us. We stood there gazing out at the night sky, taking in the bright lights of the Eiffel Tower, Sacre Coeur,

Champs Elysée and Notre Dame. After some time, the low hum of shuffling tourists stopped. I looked around to find we had the whole viewing platform to ourselves, side by side, arms linked, taking Paris in. Then mom turned to me and simply said,

"Thankyou."

Lauren Love

Thank you For the Music 2009

The three of us headed to Moreton Hall in Castletown, the old Capital of the Isle of Man. There was going to be a buffet, bring your own drinks, Abba tribute night. Mom was rubbing her hands thinking about the buffet and Patricia was choosing a comfortable shoe ready for a dance. I was hoping it wasn't going to be rubbish. One of my class ladies, Violet, was the main organiser of the event. Knowing I had my mom and auntie staying, she suggested we all come along. It was a very modest affair, the opposite of the Viking festival concert. It was in a small hall with tables and chairs taking me back to the days of school dinners, a small dance floor and stage for the band. 'We are going to be home early' I thought to myself as we walked in. Looking around there was an eclectic mix starting to fill the hall; from teenage to elderly, from fully abled to disabled mentally or physically. As soon as the music started to play, the differences between us all evaporated. Mom had never been one to get up and dance. Patricia had often tried to coax her onto the dancefloor at works parties without success. But tonight, she decided to give it a go, nothing fancy, looking a little uncomfortable stepping from side to side in time with the music, for several songs' duration. I kept taking her hand to dance with just her, knowing Patricia was quite happy dancing with the friendly strangers on the dancefloor. Mom smiled and seemed to relax whenever I did this.

We ate and nattered, and the evening whizzed by so fast, before we knew it, the band were announcing their last song as midnight approached. Mom stood up, looked down at me and Patricia and said,

"Come on, let's dance again!" We looked at each other stunned, following her onto the dancefloor. The whole room formed a circle holding hands above our heads, swaying in time to 'Thank you for the music' singing at the top of our voices. I looked sideways at mom and for the first time tonight and in all my life, she looked totally carefree.

Lauren Love

Tattoos in Ibiza 2010

This year I joined Mom and Patricia on their foreign holiday. They had been to this same resort, Santa Eulalia, this same Hotel even, twice before and loved it, so why not a third time. They wanted to show me the sights. We took the mile long walk to the markets that would be there today. We had the many obligatory bench stops along the way, posing for photographs in our oversized sunhats, one photo forever to be dubbed 'the three sombreros.'

When we approached the markets, I said I would like to buy Patrick a souvenir but didn't know what. Mom said there was a man who drew sketches which Patrick would love. I couldn't think of anything worse than sitting whilst somebody drew me, but swept along by mom's enthusiasm, within a few minutes I found myself sat in front of the easel. Mom and Patricia went off to look around the other stalls but kept returning to look how my portrait was coming along. My blonde hair was the longest it had ever been, reaching my shoulder blades. My face was makeup free as was my preference, The

119

artist had his back to passing holidaymakers, so they could see his work. For what felt like an eternity, I sat as still as I could with no change in facial expression as mom would keep appearing making 'ooh' and 'aww' sounds and at one point exaggeratedly miming the word 'beautiful' to me. I remained statuesque through all this until, from a nearby stall, I heard Patricia say to mom,

"So, are we going to get these tattoos done then?" I nearly fell off my chair! My portrait was not what I expected, beautiful but looked like a twelve-year-old version of me that would make Patrick laugh if nothing else. Mom and Patricia appeared in far less time than it would take for even one of them to have a tattoo. They were beaming from ear to ear as they pointed to the henna butterflies on their arms. They were just brilliant together.

We headed back to the hotel and sat by the pool. Mom said she was thirsty and was going to have an orange juice and lemonade. One of the bar staff approached us and I ordered half a lager.

"Make it three," said mom. And so, we spent the rest of the afternoon lounging by the pool like lager louts.

We had a siesta in our rooms, showered and changed before heading down for our evening meal. The food was good, plenty of choice to serve yourself to. We all loved not cooking. Patricia could never decide what to have when faced with a buffet, so she appeared with a jumble of small portions of everything on her plate. Mom said

"Yuk" rolling her eyes.

After our meal, we moved to a table outside by the pool, the entertainment was setting up; bingo followed by a singer. As soon as the bingo cards had been handed out Mom and Patricia, along with everyone else, burst into a ditty that was obviously familiar to them all,

"B, I, N, G, O,   B, I, N, G, O,   B, I, N, G, O... My jaw dropped, they burst out laughing, I joined in. I just loved being with these two lovely, crazy people.

I Thought We Had Years

Lauren Love

Image and Style 2011

I had got to know a lady called Leslie who was a self-employed image and style consultant. She ran group workshops in my fitness studio for my class members and it had always been a roaring success. It was a bit of a giggle and left us all feeling uplifted with a bit more idea of what clothes, make up, jewellery and hairstyle would suit us best as individuals. At every workshop I thought, 'I know who would love this.'

When they were next over, I arranged a session just for the two of them. Patricia was told the best colour shade for her was 'cool,' mom was 'warm.' I had already been told previously that I was bloody 'muted'! Leslie went on to show them the best clothes shapes to suit their figures; sleeve lengths, hemline lengths, shape of neck-lines, whether their hair would suit them better short, long, straight, or wavy. I wasn't sure what mom was making of it all, she had never had anyone pay her so much attention. Little did I know it was firing up her teenage passion for fashion and make up. I had seen photos of her up to and including her wedding day, she had a look of Mary Quant, classy, timeless, and beautiful. As we left Leslie said,

"Don't save anything for best because every day you should look your best." Mom took her literally. From that day, every single day, she looked fabulous, usually just trousers and top but the right shape, length, and shade. Always set off with great accessories, shimmering lip gloss and a touch of mascara. Every time I turned up at mom's flat, she would be standing at the top of the stairs.

"Baby!" she said lovingly, greeting me with open arms. I would give her a hug and tell her,

"You look delicious." Then with a cheeky glint in her eye, and a shuffle of the shoulders, her response would be,

"I know."

Lauren Love

Photoshoot 2012

Isobel and John ran the Whistle Stop Coffee Shop, where today they were hosting a charity auction. None of the lots so far had been of interest to me, including the current one, a photoshoot day with a local well-established photographer. Patrick popped his head over my shoulder.

"Place a bid" he suggested.

"Why would I? I don't like having my photo taken." I responded with a confused whisper.

"It would be a great present for your mom and auntie Patricia." Patrick had the best ideas. In a heartbeat my disinterest turned to a need to have the winning bid. It was my lucky day.

I sent a copy of the voucher to mom in her birthday card and a few months later they were with us again, full of excitement about our photoshoot day. The photographer, Daniel had issued us with a few rules. We were all to wear the same light colour tops, plain, no patterns. We got ready that morning, each of us taking much longer in the bathroom than ever before. We

125

agreed we would wear dark trousers and a cream top. I chose a thin fluffy cream jumper. Patricia came downstairs in a cream cotton top with lacey sleeves. Then mom appeared with her favourite cream sweatshirt embossed with a giant black glittery butterfly ... she didn't do rules.

Daniel was very laid back and good fun. I had told him the photoshoot was for mom's birthday, so he made a fuss of 'the birthday girl' but played Patricia up all the way through the shoot as well. He suggested individual poses at first, achieving a serene look from me, a contented shot of Patricia and a smile which failed to hide stifled giggles from mom. At the end of the afternoon, he positioned the three of us together, with the chestnut-haired birthday girl and her large glittery butterfly in the centre, flanked by the blondies, me and Patricia turning in towards her. The pose perfectly capturing not just mother with daughter and sister, but the best of friends having a ball. And the butterfly by the way, set that photo off a treat.

Lauren Love

Custody of the Sofa 2012

L ater that same year mom and Patricia came over for Christmas. For the last few years, we had a new sofa and mom loved it. The upholstery was a plush oatmeal and it seemed to hug you as soon as you sat on it. Every time she came over, she made a beeline for it. Unbeknown to me, Patrick had sellotaped an A4 note to it, reading 'Hands Off My Sofa!' We walked into the lounge put the cases down and while we were all laughing at the note, mom whipped it off, cheekily saying,

"I don't think so," falling into the sofa and stretching out. She budged up a bit when Patrick came home, so they could share it.

We were all having a cosy night in a few days before Christmas. Mom had her annual glass of baileys in hand, Patricia a white wine, me and Patrick a bottle of lager. We were watching 'It's a Wonderful Life', mine and mom's favourite Christmas film. She just loved the character Clarence, a hapless second-class angel with the faith of a child, who had been passed over for his wings for the past 200 years. She often saw a heron on her riverbank walk near her flat back home and had named him Clarence. Whenever we were together, and heard a bell ring, we would share a glance and quietly say in unison,

"Every time a bell rings, an angel gets his wings." The most famous line in the film. When I offered to top mom's glass up, she insisted she would do it, while I got the other drinks. When she sat back down, enveloped by the sofa, Patrick looked over at her glass

"You got enough there?" he chuckled.

"Yep" came the cheeky reply. Mom's home measure was about four pub measures. It had only just turned nine o'clock when she suddenly stood up and announced,

"I'm pissed, I'm going to bed." The three of us couldn't stop laughing as she gingerly walked upstairs with a big grin on her face.

A couple of nights after Christmas mom had fallen asleep on 'her' sofa and the rest of us decided we would head for bed. I gentle rocked her shoulder, she stirred very sleepily

"We are heading to bed now mom, are you coming?"

"Erm, in a bit" she said snuggling back down. That night Patrick started to snore, and I could not drop off, so I grabbed the fold up guest mattress and took it downstairs where mom was still in a deep sleep. As I put my bed together, she did not stir. It was only once I'd settled, I realised mom was snoring louder than Patrick! So, I gently woke her again, she was in such a deep sleep, but she forced herself into a sitting then standing position. As she padded past me, with eyes barely open, she stopped, turned, and said in the sleepiest slur,

"Shall I tuck you in?" I was on the floor so that would not have been an easy task even when fully awake but my heart burst with her offer.

"No, I'm fine mom, it's a bit low down here, you get off to bed, we'll have a big hug in the morning"

"Ok ni, night" she mumbled already padding away from me.

I Thought We Had Years

First Step of the Return 2013

Eventually we left the Isle of Man when Patrick got a work transfer to Alston, Cumbria. We rented a little house in a quaint village called Melmerby. A month later, the train pulled into Platform One at Penrith and what a sight to behold when the terrible twosome came tumbling out with their cases.

"That was a lovely train journey" Patricia declared, having spotted me. Mom was trailing behind rolling her eyes

"She talks to anyone, I don't know what she finds to talk about." They were making me laugh before I had even reached them. We hugged and kissed, and I took a couple of their bags while they each wheeled their case behind them. When we reached the foot of the stairs that led to the carpark, I took Patricia's case off her and mom started the ascent with hers. I popped the case at the top and turned back down to take mom's. But she had noticed an elderly lady struggling with her own case and said to her,

"Don't worry my daughter will help you." Which I duly did, while mom looked on as proud as punch.

As I drove into Melmerby, I pointed out the six things of interest in the village, knowing already which one they would love the most; The Bakery and Café, Traditional Wooden Toy Shop, Tiny Village Store, The Shepherds Inn Pub, The Man who sat on the cobblestone arched bridge every afternoon spotting red squirrels and La Brocante (a barn full of second-hand goods.) The latter was only open on Fridays and Saturdays. As I thought mom and Patricia couldn't wait for Friday to come around, then having to revisit on Saturday. It was an Aladdin's Cave and we spent most of the weekend browsing in there.

The writing was on the wall as soon as we walked into the Carpenter's Toy Shop. I put a 50p in the slot on the wall and told them to look up as the handmade train started to chugg along the track that ran around the perimeter of the shop, above head height. Mom left the shop armed with bags full of Christmas presents for all the children in the family, which was still four months away. We returned the next day to buy more gifts she had been thinking about all night. I was always telling her she should live in Lapland and change her name to Mrs Christmas.

As for the old, bearded man who sat on the cobblestone bridge spotting red squirrels, he seemed to disappear that week. Someone must have told him the terrible twosome were in town.

I Thought We Had Years

Lauren Love

A Manic Christmas 2013

Only five months later, Patrick had another work transfer which brought us a tiny bit closer to Birmingham, so we found ourselves living smack bang in the middle of the Honeypot of Bowness on Windermere. In the middle of the move, we drove to mom for Christmas dinner. Ben had cooked a lovely meal for the four of us, but I was caught off guard to find mom in the throes of a manic episode. She played Christmas music so loud we couldn't hear each other without shouting. There was a large light up star on the dining table that kept changing colour and flashing at a fast pace. I remembered what the psychiatric doctors had always said so I changed the CD to one with Christmas ballads, turning the volume down while I was at it. I asked her if I could switch off the flashing star, faking a brooding headache. She laughed loudly when Ben played around, and she simply couldn't sit still. She wore a bright red tracksuit and Christmas antlers in her unwashed hair and the most worrying sign of all, she looked days past overtired.

For the first time, the relentless questions spinning around in my head were not berating: Why now? Twenty years since she was last in hospital apart from the two weeks self-admittance when nan died; Fifteen years since dad left. It doesn't make sense, something's different this time. I returned to Bowness, my head swimming with the shock of it. I had become so complacent. I could see how much happier she had become without dad and since Ben had moved in. I had convinced myself she would never be unwell again, with medication of course but …… and then it hit me. Way back in April, Ben had looked into the medication she was on and was concerned about the affect they had on kidney function. Mom knew the side effects as did I, she had blood tests every six months for as long as I could remember to check on her kidney and liver function. She was feeling so well, so much like her old self that she wondered if she still needed the depixol injection every four weeks. I remembered her calling me, having asked for an appointment with her psychiatric doctor. He strongly advised her against stopping the medication, as she had 'Chronic' Manic Depression and so it was too big a risk to take. In other words, when she was poorly, she was very poorly, for a very long time. I told mom that I agreed with the doctor that it was not worth the risk, reminding her, as if she needed reminding, how hard it had been for her every time she had been in hospital and of the barbaric electric shock treatment she had undergone. I totally understood Ben's logic, he was concerned about her 'physicals' when her 'mentals' seemed all good now, as he put it. He felt frustrated with mom, mostly down to her lifestyle and medical condition which he later admitted he had no real understanding of, saying he massively mistakenly thought 'oh, you can pull your socks up and come out of that!' Although I wanted her to live to the ripest of ripe old ages, I didn't want her to end her days on a psychiatric ward, she would have hated that. I didn't want her to have to go into one of those places ever again and was convinced she never would, she was so well now and had been for so many years.

So, mom came to a compromise between the advice of the doctor, Ben and me, by very slightly reducing her depixol injection dosage, she was already on a very low dose of 80ml, it was to be reduced to 70ml and see how it goes. Depixol acts as a reservoir and the body draws on it as it needs it, maintaining equilibrium of an otherwise chemical imbalance in the brain. So of course, it was feasible that it had taken these last eight months before any adverse effects materialised. So, Ben made an appointment for mom to have her depixol injection early, increasing to the previous long term 80ml dose. It did the trick, over the next four- or five-months mom's mania subsided very slowly, without the low that usually followed. We were all so relieved, none more than mom, but we should have known better. The low always followed the high.

I Thought We Had Years

Lauren Love

The Camera Never Lies 2014

id I notice mom was still a little hyper over three months later? Yes, I did, but she was only a little bubbly now, nobody else would have noticed. It was a party, Patricia's seventieth birthday, she was mingling with her family, having a good time. Besides which I suppose subconsciously I was just relieved that after more than three months, there had not been the usual inevitable low. Mom looked lovely in a cream lacey boho style blouse and black trousers. Her hair was no longer her usual chestnut after her hairdresser of the last thirty years, had suggested she try going blonde. She agreed as long as it was a salt and pepper blonde. She happily posed while I took photos of her hugging her auntie May and Patrick. Towards the end of the evening Patrick took a photo of us two with mom holding flowers and me holding balloon animals. Ben was not there and this time it was not because of Derek. Now that Derek kept his distance, inviting him was not even a consideration for Patricia.

"I feel bad that Ben hasn't come" mom quietly told me.

"He's a grown man mom, you can't make him come and Patricia knows that" I responded.

"I know, but it's bad that he isn't here for her seventieth," she said sadly. Our conversation was cut short when mom's cousin John coincidentally asked her "How's Ben doing Dette?" John was the only one who called her Dette, I thought it was lovely. There was no side to him so mom happily, proudly, chatted to him about Ben, forgetting her embarrassment about his absence.

I got the photos printed, put the one of mom and Patrick in a frame for us, and two copies of the one of mom and May for each of them. As soon as mom opened hers, she placed it on the nest of tables next to her two-seater sofa.

"I look quite nice on that photo" she said. I agreed, but then I looked a little closer at the photo and realised she looked tired, bone deep tired. I had no idea why, but I suddenly felt so very sad. The heart knows what it knows even when the brain can't bear to process it.

Lauren Love

Beatrix Potter Easter 2014

I picked Mom and Patricia up from Windermere train station just a few days after Patricia's party. I couldn't wait to show them the sights but was annoyed that I hadn't been able to get time off work at Ambleside Post Office. Easter was one of the busiest times and it was short notice so the only way I was going to get any time off was if I quit my job or feigned illness. Obviously, I was too much of a goody two shoes to do either of those things.

I only had two full days with them on my days off. We went to The World of Beatrix Potter. Patricia loved Jemima Puddle duck, mom's favourite was Hunca Munca the mouse, while I had a soft spot for Mrs Tiggy Winkle. We stood out like sore thumbs without young children in tow and didn't care one bit. The following day we headed to Hilltop Farm the home of Beatrix Potter. Her writing desks were still in place in the downstairs sitting room and a hilltop tourist guide was reading Beatrix Potter stories upstairs as all the young children sat listening wide eyed. We listened outside the door, spellbound for some time ourselves.

Most days they had to spend finding their own way around, but they would always get the bus to Ambleside to meet me in my lunch break. We would sit on the bench right outside, so we didn't waste any time. I hated going back to work, but I needed the job until I.built my exercise classes up again.

One of those lunchtimes towards the end of their visit, mom was so quiet, not quite 'with it'. Patricia noticed too. I was so glad they had each other, she always looked out for her but that afternoon on the post office I could not think of anything other than mom. I was still struggling to process the pattern of mom's recent setback as it had been so drawn out this time.

On the day they were due to leave, my friend Ellen and her family were due to arrive for a couple of days. I thought mom would enjoy seeing her again as it had been a while, but she became even quieter. As I carried their cases out to my car ready to head to the train station I said,

"You haven't seen Ellen for years have you mom, I'm glad you got to see her before you left", but she gazed at me, and sounding so worried, said,

"It's too much, it's just too much for you." When I got back to the house, I asked Ellen if she thought there was anything wrong with mom. She said she hadn't noticed. It brought me no comfort; I couldn't shake it.

"Something's not right" I said, almost to myself, as the bad penny finally dropped.

Lauren Love

Youngest on the Ward May 2014

One year and one month after that small reduction in depixol injection, mom had gone through every stage; manic episode, inability to sleep, racing mind, low mood, clinical depression and now she had slipped away from us into a catatonic state.

We had just pulled up in mom's Grove, Patrick gave me a hug knowing Ben and Patricia were already with mom so, he was just dropping me off to give us all time together. Before I had shut the car door, dad appeared standing right in front of us, clearly agitated. I felt precious time passing me by as he relayed what had just happened. He said he had been to mom's and Ben had started a physical fight with him. I was a bit stunned by his sudden appearance. Although I had told him mom wasn't well over the phone and that I was travelling down from Windermere today, I didn't expect to see him here. He very rarely saw mom these days. All I could think was 'I need to get to mom.' It felt very strange, at the very time we were all so worried about her, he seemed to suddenly want attention. I had never seen him so upset, so I gave him a hug and said I would be in touch. Patrick hurried things along for me and dad drove off.

Mom was sat on the edge of her two-seater sofa, eyes bulging, face gaunt, she looked exhausted and frightened. She wasn't speaking. Patricia and Ben were there. I always tried to be strong for mom, but the sight of her broke me. I knelt on the floor, by her feet, my hands on her lap and I couldn't stop my tears.

"Oh Mom, how can we help you, what can we do?" I knew it was a stupid question, I knew there was nothing we could do, not now.

"It's as if I'm in a cocoon, no-one can get in and I can't get out. It's so lonely in here. B"

For a few moments her fixed gaze was turned towards me, the look in her eyes changing from fear to sadness, she was looking straight into my soul and I hers. I knew she was trapped inside her own head and there was nothing I could do. My heart was bursting with so much love for her, so much hopeless, helpless love.

Ben started to tell me what had happened with dad, saying he had told him he couldn't come in as mom wasn't well, but dad barged his way in anyway. Dad went straight over to mom's bureau in the lounge where she had always kept any paperwork. Ben asked what he thought he was doing, but dad didn't answer as he continued to rifle through letters. Ben made dad leave. Patricia arrived shortly after. They both said he must have been looking through the bureau for something related to money, that mom being unwell again was going to affect' payday.' I couldn't take it in, I couldn't take my eyes off mom.   That afternoon I stayed with mom after Patricia had left, to give Ben some time to get out and have a break.   Patrick came back and brought mom a McDonalds cheeseburger, no salad, no gherkins as she liked it.   It hadn't occurred to me that he had never seen mom unwell because she hadn't been unwell in all the years we had been together. He handed her the burger, I unwrapped it telling her it was as she liked it no gherkins, no salad because,

"You don't like all that stuff do you mom?" I couldn't believe it when she took a bite saying

"Hate it" the first words she had said in the last twenty-four hours. I assume she meant gherkins etc as she ate the entire burger. Patrick left the room. I went into the kitchen to make us all a drink to find my six foot two, broad shouldered husband crying.

"That's the saddest thing I've ever seen, I don't know how you cope" he said while wrapping his arms around me.

Patricia and Ben washed her, dressed her, held her up while she walked from lounge to bedroom to bathroom for a few more days. Beds on psychiatric wards were sparse and they were only offering us hospitals hundreds of miles away. Until after just a few days a space became available at Moseley. Having turned sixty-five just two months ago, mom was classed as geriatric and was now living on a ward with dementia patients who would never get any better. I don't know why this bothered me, but it did. I travelled down to stay with Patricia telling Patrick I may not return, knowing I would not be able to come away from her again while she was so ill. I did not return to Windermere and while Patrick saw out the last two months of our lease and served his notice at work, I looked for a place to live and work in Birmingham, whilst staying with Patricia.

I walked onto the ward and found mom sitting in her bedroom, she still was not speaking. I told her I would not be going back to Windermere, that we would always stay close now and I answered the question I know she wished she was able to ask.

"I will not allow them to give you shock treatment mom, I promise you." The treatment she was given was very different this time, I guess medicine had progressed in the last twenty years, so it could only be a good thing. But her behaviour was different this time, she had several psychotic episodes which she had never experienced before. The day Leigh visited her, her precious granddaughter, mom was sat in the corridor, watching everything and everyone, both hands clasping Leigh's hand, holding it tight, telling her she must go, that her and her baby were not safe here. Leigh was not pregnant.

The day I found somewhere to live for me and Patrick and a job that came with it, I couldn't wait to tell mom. I found her in her bedroom, she was still hardly speaking after a month. I excitedly told her how we would be living on a lovely farm near Balsall Common only a twenty-minute drive away from her and how the nice lady on the farm needed domestic help, meaning I had paid work too. I could hear myself keep repeating that I would always be close by now and how we could see each other all the time when she comes home. She looked confused and sad and then uttered the first words she had spoken to me in weeks,

"Cleaning? but you're so clever."

Mom stayed on that ward from May to October. The hospital hadn't updated their records and didn't realise that mom and dad had been separated for the past fifteen years. The day I walked in to be immediately asked into the staff office, they were full of apologies. They said that it was due to their mistake in sending out a letter to him that he had visited her, in her bedroom. I don't know what alerted them to this mistake but that day and for a while afterwards mom's progress slipped back. The only words she spoke to me for weeks after were,

"He looked at me like he hated me." I had told dad, back in May, that we had taken mom to hospital and that she was being looked after and I was back in Birmingham. I didn't tell him which hospital as I was pretty sure mom would not want him to visit. I also considered it all hypothetical as he rarely visited her in hospital when they were living together as a married couple. Shortly after that, I received a text from dad saying,

"Due to being kept out of the loop, I am now considerably worse off." Patrick who had always played devil's advocate trying to keep family together, finally snapped saying dad didn't deserve me. I had defended him against the 'bureau rifling incident' saying it was not money related, that he genuinely seemed concerned for mom. Reading that text knocked the wind out of me as he proved everyone else right and me naïve. He had been claiming carers allowance for mom and got her to claim carers allowance for his mom and she was to pass it on to him. I remembered her telling me about it shortly after he left her, that she was not comfortable with it, that she knew it was wrong and she was worried she would get into trouble for it. But she couldn't face standing up to him and she didn't want me to say anything as it would come back on her. I can only guess dad's text to me had something to do with this. I never got to the bottom of it as I didn't want to cause mom any further stress and dad's last text made me not want anything more to do with him, whatever it related to. Clearly his main concern and annoyance was that his income had reduced, while mom was so unwell yet again. How could mom's circumstance, who he left fifteen years ago affect his income? She hadn't seen or heard from him for the last few years.

By September with little improvement in mom's recovery and doctors' meetings with me and Ben involving suggestions of shock treatment and power of attorney, I became worried. She had always come back to me; she would do it again right? Not knowing if it was the totally right or totally wrong thing to do, I knelt at her feet as I had that day in her flat, with my hands on her lap.

"They say you're not getting any better, they say they have tried everything, I told them you do not want shock treatment, but you have to get better mom, we need you home with us." She never said a word but slowly each visit every other day I saw an improvement, so slight anyone other than a daughter desperate to see it, would not have noticed. She was strong and she was doing it, she would be coming home.

I Thought We Had Years

Turning A Corner September 2014

The phone rang, it was twenty to nine in the evening. "Lauren?"

"Speaking" I replied, not recognising the voice I hadn't heard for six months.

"It's me, your mom, I've turned a corner." came her beautiful joy filled words. I began to cry; I couldn't believe it. I handed the phone to Patrick repeating what she had said to me, letting him talk to her for a moment while I pulled myself together. The next day I could not wait to get to her and found her sat in the courtyard garden. I sat next to her on the bench and listened to this extraordinary, brave woman tell me what had been going on inside her own head this past year; six months before going into hospital until now. She spoke calmly often pausing as if reflecting and I just listened, allowing her the power of silence as she had done for me so many times.

On leaving the ward that day, one of the nurses stopped me to tell me my mom was one of the loveliest people they had ever met. She said mom had lifted all their spirits as they never saw anybody get better normally. She was the first non-dementia patient they had nursed and meeting the 'real her' had brought them so much joy. I was so proud of her and felt so lucky that she was my mom.

It wasn't plain sailing after that, she slipped back a little, but by the end of October, we walked through the doors of the hospital hand in hand, with discharge papers.

"Thank you, Lauren, I don't think I would ever have got out of there if it wasn't for you and Ben." I squeezed her hand and as we walked to the car, I knew I couldn't bear to let go of her ever again.

Lauren Love

Mrs Christmas November 2014

It was a cold, wet November day, so me and mom had to force ourselves off her sofa to head over to Newington Clinic. Mom's flat, as she always called it, was actually a first-floor maisonette which overlooked Marston Green Park. This gave her a lovely view of a large play area for the local kids and masses of open greenery with meandering paths. To the left of the park was a housing estate built twenty years ago, and Newington was nestled in a corner of this estate. To walk there would have taken us about twenty-five minutes but it was a miserable day outside. So, at quarter to three we prised ourselves from the cosiness of snuggling up together on the sofa with a cup of coffee to my little red Citroën, Cybill, in the car park at the end of the grove. Whenever we came out of the local Asda with a trolley full of groceries, mom would say with a big grin,

"Where's that Cybill." We never could remember where we had parked her.

On the short drive to this first consultation mom was quieter than normal. That did not worry me because she had always been quiet but when she did speak it was usually with warmth or cheekiness, but today she seemed serious, a little worried even.

"Do you want me to come in with you when the doctor calls you through mom?" I asked gently.

"Yes." came the short reply.

"Is there anything you want to tell the doctor or ask him?"

"Don't know" she shrugged

"I think you seem ok, with the meds you are on, do you?"

"Mm" she replied reluctantly. In the forty years she had suffered with this illness, she had never talked about it. She said talking about it made it more intense. I didn't like to push her, but I wanted to make sure she was on the right track with the medication she was on. In addition to her usual long standing depixol injection, they had kept her on another anti-psychotic pill which they introduced at Moseley Hospital. This, they said would be reduced and eventually stopped altogether, leaving just the injection. This was what we wanted too but we had to get the timing right. Even changing the dose of the depixol was so hard to judge timing wise, as it worked like a reservoir, with the body drawing on it for a long-term stabilising effect. So, any changes in the dose would not take effect for several months, as we knew only too well.

We arrived at Newington, signed in and the receptionist let us through to the waiting room. It didn't feel like a waiting room, more like a communal lounge with free drinks machines, offering water, coffee tea or hot chocolate. We sat quietly, opposite a young man, mid-twenties probably, but he looked jaded which made him look older. All I could see out of the corner of my eye was his leg twitching up and down constantly and his forefinger and thumb making fast small strokes on the hem of his jacket. A young man who would be in his prime if it wasn't for his own mind holding him back and weighing him down. Mom always described her illness as 'an invisible worm' …

"My most favourite poem.

The Sick Rose

O Rose, thou art sick
The invisible worm
That flies in the night
In the howling storm:
Has found out thy bed
Of crimson joy
And his dark secret love
Does thy life destroy
William Blake. B"

A young, tall, dark, well-dressed man with a kind smile and a close shaven black beard appeared from one of the hallways into the centre of the lounge, looking over at us.

"Bernadette?" it was nice how he didn't bother with her surname, more personal. Mom stood up

"Hello" she said softly, then turned to me to follow her. Just a few steps down the hallway, Dr Brad as we would come to call him, buzzed through a security door and then directly into a room on the right. A small, but light and airy office. He closed the door behind us and offered us a seat while asking mom how she was and then who I was in relation. I could tell mom liked this new doctor and I did too. He took his time, he listened, he cared and crucially he had a sense of humour. He asked all the necessary questions to acquire the information he needed to decide whether mom was on the right track, but he interspersed them with tales of his own family. It felt like a chat with a concerned friend rather than a formal consultation with a doctor, it almost felt odd that he didn't offer us a cup of tea.

"So, Bernadette, if you are happy, we could have a longer gap until we next meet, say in two months?" Mom looked over at me

"What do you think Lauren?" I tried not to say anything in the consultations unless I was specifically asked by mom or the doctor, I answered looking at mom, rather than Dr Brad.

"Well, do you think we should keep it to one month this time because that will be just before Christmas and you can sometimes find it hard to sleep coming up to Christmas, can't you?"

"Yes, sometimes" mom said quietly. I turned to Dr Brad,

"Mom is known as 'Mrs Christmas' because she loves buying presents for everyone. "I smiled over at mom, she smiled back at me, and then cheekily at Dr Brad. "You can get a bit caught up in the excitement of it all can't you Mom?" Mom nodded. "I think what probably happens is you are lying awake at night thinking about what you have bought and what presents you still want to get for everybody and then you find it hard to sleep. Plus, you are toing and froing to the shops more to buy them and it can all have a bit of a snowball effect sometimes, can't it?" I suggested to her.

"Yes, I do find it takes me longer to get to sleep when I'm thinking about what presents to buy, I love it" said mom, apologetic yet excited all at once. I added,

"The thing is lack of sleep is always a warning sign and I worry because I know mom doesn't necessarily tell me when she's not sleeping, do you mom?"

"Well, you worry too much" she said quietly looking down at her lap.

"Ok," said Dr Brad "how about I prescribe you some sleeping tablets ..."

"Oh no, I don't want more pills and I don't want to get addicted to them" mom insisted.

"Ok, I understand what you're saying Bernadette, but I would only prescribe you three tablets, so they are there as a safety net and you would only take one of them if you really could not sleep on any given night. But it's important that you take it on the first night you cannot sleep, to get your sleep patterns back on track straight away. As you only have three tablets it is impossible for you to become addicted." There was a bit of a tumbleweed moment. "What do you think?" he asked. Mom and I looked at each other, I was just about to put my two penneth in again when she sat taller, beamed from ear to ear and said,

"Yes ... that's a good idea." I saw Dr Brad smile warmly to himself as he turned to enter the details into his computer. Then turning back,

"Ok Bernadette so I will see you in one month's time, just before Christmas. If you make an appointment at reception. Lovely to meet you." We all stood and while I opened the office door and he shook mom's hand, I heard her say,

"I love your beard doctor."

"Oh, thank you" he chuckled, as his hand went to his chin. We walked the few steps along the hallway to the security door that led into the lounge and reception area. I pressed the green button and as I stood side on holding the door open for mom, I looked back and watched Dr Brad walking back into his office, his hand still stroking his chin and his smile lingering. I thought how hard his job must be and how mom must be like a breath of fresh air.

A few days later while mom and I were back in our favourite place, snuggled up on her sofa, I approached the 'C' word.

"So where do you want to go to do your Christmas present shopping?"

"I'm going to get everyone vouchers this year" she said positively. I nearly fell off the sofa. I had never known mom give vouchers unless it was in addition to a present, never in place of. Even when we were kids and she had no money of her own, she would scrimp and scrape, saving a couple of pounds every week all through the year for birthdays and Christmas. The £40 weekly grocery money for the four of us never went as far as she needed it to, always putting something to one side at the till as we watched the total going over our budget.

"Vouchers, that's a great idea, I think I might do the same it will save a lot of time shopping and wrapping, won't it?" I was so relieved and amazed; I knew how hard a decision this would have been for her.

"Well, it will stop me getting carried away and stopping me sleeping won't it." She sounded a little disappointed but adamant. One thing I knew for sure, when she made her mind up about something there was no swaying her.

"Yep, we can have a nice chillout instead" I replied chirpily, knowing that for mom, present shopping was second only to chilling out. She had obviously thought about what was discussed at the consultation and had decided she was going to take matters into her own hands. I was so in awe of her strength. Mrs Christmas buying everybody vouchers, this was worthy of sponsorship like running a marathon or climbing Everest. I could see that, but to anyone else it was nothing out of the ordinary.

One week and one day before Christmas we were back at Newington, sitting opposite Dr Brad.

"So, Bernadette, I remember you are called Mrs Christmas" Instantly mom jumped in,

"No" all serious and about to offer her actual surname. I laughed,

"No, remember mom, we told Dr Brad how we say you should be called Mrs Christmas because you love buying presents?"

"Oh yes" she said a little embarrassed. "Well, I've given everyone vouchers this year" she told him "I didn't want to have to use the sleeping pill and I didn't want to risk it" she continued.

"And have you slept well since I last saw you?"

"Yes, I have, I still have the three pills you gave me in my kitchen cupboard" she answered happily.

"That's good news Bernadette, but you know it is fine to use them one at a time if you need to?" he gently assured her. She nodded. He then went on to ask her about her eating, drinking, and sleeping habits. He had already established that she was not a drinker, having the occasional baileys or cherry b at Christmas at the very most and that her eating habits needed improvement, not that she ate too much just the wrong things sometimes.

"And your sleeping pattern, Bernadette, what's that like? … what time would you normally get up?"

"Late" she said sheepishly "about eleven … sometimes later" she added.

"And what time would you normally go to bed at night?"

"Usually, I go to bed with a bottle about ten o'clock" Dr Brad's eyes opened wide, and he tried to sound as calm as possible as he asked,

"And what would it be, wine?" me and mom burst out laughing and said in unison,

"No, a hot water bottle." His whole body seemed to relax, and he found himself beaming from ear to ear once again.

Christmas Day dinner was cooked and enjoyed at the flat me and Patrick had been renting since June of that year on the farm. The only downfall was it had the tiniest kitchen you have ever seen, so organising dinner for the four of us was a challenge. It was a perfect day, so different from twelve months ago. Mom was relaxed, it was the first time Ben had come to the farm. He loved it and mom loved that he loved it. Patrick was always more comfortable entertaining in our own home rather than being the guest. Everyone was relaxed, happy and well. I liked living and cleaning at the farm, the family were kind and allowed me flexibility to visit mom and attend doctors' meetings whenever I needed to. It was perfect and mom could see that now. Mine and Patrick's life had changed so much these last eighteen months, leaving our home and businesses behind but as we all sat down to Christmas dinner that day, I realised it had all been more than worth it. This was exactly as it should be.

I Thought We Had Years

Another Twist of the Knife 2015

Mom felt sad that I had no contact with dad anymore, she said I should have my dad in my life. She felt the same about Ben but had long given up any hope of a reconciliation between them. I said as time passed, we would probably be in contact and left it at that. She looked doubtful.

"Don't you think we are all better off without him mom?" I asked her.

"I am" she replied "but that doesn't mean you and Ben shouldn't have your dad in your life"

"Well, if it's meant to be, he will meet us halfway won't he." I said. She looked even more doubtful. We were walking towards Asda when I saw him.

"There's dad "I said pointing right at him as he walked towards us. As we both said hello, he looked directly at mom, looking through her and carried on walking past us, brushing past mom's shoulder. We stopped and looked back, he just carried on walking. Mom was quiet the rest of that afternoon and after we had unpacked her shopping and sat with a cup of tea in her flat, she finally said,

"After thirty-two years of marriage you would think he would at least say hello when he passes me in the street"

Lauren Love

The Circle of Life 2016

I was driving me and mom down to join Patricia at her static caravan in Lowestoft. Ben had taken mom to see May in hospital just a few days before. May could barely breath now, having suffered with emphysema for years. Mom and Patricia thought the world of May, they looked up to her like a big sister rather than an auntie as she was twelve years younger than their mom Lucy. Mom advised me not to visit her before we left as she was struggling to try to speak when she was at her bedside. Patricia would visit her as soon as we all returned from the caravan in four days' time.

The evening after we arrived, while mulling over the menu in the clubhouse, Patricia received a call from her cousin James, May's youngest son. We all knew there was only one reason he would have phoned, so we headed out into a quiet spot near the foyer. The three of us held each other, standing in a tight circle, without a word. At first, I felt like I was imposing on their shared grief, but as they held each other and me tighter, I realised we had all lost a big part of us. They had lost the last of their parents' generation, the last of their roots. I kept hearing May's voice telling me she had a lot of faith in me just a few months ago, I never knew why she said it, but it stayed with me. May had been with mom the day I was born. She had delivered the first part of me into this world. Now she had been taken from it. The circle of life dawning on me for the first time.

Lauren Love

Life's Good Autumn 2016

Sitting on the park bench, side by side, the two of us were chatting about nothing in particular, soaking up being together.

"You're a happy little soul, aren't you?" I said squeezing her hand. Her eyes lit up her face. Her smile was so sweet and serene, she gave a little nod.

"Life's good" she said. When writing in the 'From Me to You' Journal that I sent her in 2010 on the page that posed the question 'What are the happiest or greatest memories in your life?' she wrote,

"Just after I had my Babies." But I believe the years 2015 – 2019 were among her happiest.

Tuesdays and Saturdays were the best days, they were our days together. I would phone her every night but, on a Monday, and Friday night the conversation would always go like this,

"What's the plan for tomorrow then Mom?"

"Well … the Plan Stan … is … a bit of shopping at Asda … and … maybe a walk." Her voice always filled with excitement about the following day, almost like a child's on Christmas Eve. So did mine, now I think about it. We almost always went to Asda for food shopping. The walking was less regular and happened after a bit of friendly persuasion from me. During the colder months, as we walked out of her door, her wearing her Paddington bear duffle coat and bright pink bobble hat, I would ask if she had everything, keys, purse, phone, after each of which she would say,

"Check" then she would pat one of her duffle coat pockets and say, "Marmalade sandwiches, check" which always made me laugh. During our walks. if anybody was sitting on the benches as we approached, she would chuckle and say,

"Bloody cheek", then she would smile at the trespasser and rhetorically ask "Room for a little one?" They would always smile & budge up. I was usually teetering on the edge of the bench until they moved on. Often, she would take the walk on her own, then her face would pop up on my phone and on answering the call I would hear,

"Guess where I am?" in her proud as punch voice.

"On the park bench" I answered, rather than asked, because I knew that was exactly where she was and felt suddenly misplaced that I wasn't sat beside her.

One Saturday in the confectionery aisle of Asda, she asked,

"Aren't you getting some wine gums for Patrick?"

"He had some last week; I don't want to encourage him" I replied.

"Poor little sod can't even have a bag of sweets" she said rolling her eyes. Later that day when I unpacked my

168

own shopping at home, I found a bag of wine gums and cinder toffee that had been placed as stowaways somewhere between the checkout and the car. That same day, we sat on the chairs at the end of the checkout tills, with our full trolleys alongside us. As we rested, a lady looked over at the two of us while we were giggling away about something or other. Her eyes seemed unable to look away and she was beaming at us. I knew what we had was rare and sometimes it seemed to make other people light up.

We chuckled like silly schoolfriends while shopping. We sang 'Busy Doing Nothing' and 'Truly Scrumptious' arm in arm, in the park, stopping to look at each other, heads thrown back as we sang the exaggerated line in each song and giggling every time. We snuggled up on the smaller of her two sofas, reaching behind us to grab blankets warmed on the radiator, listening to music. After I had been there for half an hour or more, I would say,

"Well, I tell you something, I definitely do not want a cuppa."

"Bloody good job" she would say "cos you're not bloody getting one." Then she would pop the kettle on chuckling to herself. She was right, life was good.

I Thought We Had Years

Lauren Love

Crossed Fingers Early 2018

I was covering Pilates Classes for a local instructor in Kenilworth for six weeks. I had continually worked part time as a Personal Trainer and Gym Instructor, alongside cleaning at the farm, but hadn't taught Pilates Classes since leaving the Isle of Man five years ago. I was so nervous. I was about to turn it down, but Patrick and mom encouraged me to do it, telling me I'd be great as soon as I was back in the swing. This was typical Patrick, upbeat, positive, always looking for the next opportunity for us, but not so typical of mom. If she could see I didn't want to do something she would not push me to do it, but this time she did.

The class were a tough crowd, clearly not happy at the idea of having a 'fill in' teacher for six weeks. But they soon realised, and I gradually remembered, I was a very good Pilates Teacher. Patrick and mom had been right, it had been a real confidence boost for me and though I hadn't realised it yet, it would set me on the path I needed in the nick of time. Nevertheless, I felt a little nervous at the start of each class and each week asked mom to cross her fingers for me.

On my way home from my third or fourth class, I phoned mom, as I always did to let her know how I had got on.

"How did the first ten minutes of your class go today Lauren?" she asked me eagerly.

"Ok mom, why?"

"Because I was getting our tea ready, and I forgot to cross my fingers until ten past seven."

"So, you had your fingers crossed the whole time you were eating your tea?" I asked smiling to myself, already knowing the answer.

"Yes, on both hands."

Soon after that, mom gave me a serious talking to, the only one I can remember. She was always telling me I was beautiful, and would look beautiful in a bin bag, I knew she meant all the lovely things she said to me, but I would always respond with,

"Not biased at all are you?" So it was turned into a bit of an in joke between us. But this time she would not allow me to laugh it off, she looked at me, without the hint of a smile, making sure I took in every word.

"There's nothing not to like about you because you are kind and approachable, there are not many people like you in this world and don't you ever forget it." She did not look away. I smiled shyly, coming from her it meant the world because she was the kindest person I had ever known, but then again everything good about me was because of her.

I Thought We Had Years

70th Birthday March 2018

B en arranged a family meal at The Boot pub in Lapworth for mom's seventieth birthday. There were twelve of us including Ben's ex-girlfriend Dawn (Jack and Leigh's Mom) and Dawn's other two daughters Maryam and Aminah. Mom had often visited Dawn who had been there for her over the years. Dawn had taken her to a cat breeder to buy a gorgeous grey kitten Scrumpy Joe, to keep her company. Mom treated Maryam and Aminah as her own grandchildren and Dawn loved her all the more for it.

Jack liked a drink and when the birthday cake was brought to the table for her, Jack's voice could be heard way above the rest of us singing,

"Happy birthday to my MY NANNY." Making mom giggle but blush a little. She loved having her family together but wasn't used to being the centre of attention.

I Thought We Had Years

I knew mom would love a photo of her with me and Ben. It would be the first photo of the three of us together since we were children. I always thought the best photos were those taken when the subjects were unaware, so I had asked Patrick to take one when we weren't looking. But we were sitting on opposite sides of the table, so we stood up to pose for it. Ben stood one side of her, seven inches taller, his arm around her shoulder. He wore his favourite shirt which mom had bought him, short sleeved, navy, patterned with small white birds and black jeans. His dark brown hair had a little gel in it making it spikier than normal. I stood the other side of her, four inches taller, two inches of which were due to the slim heel on my black suede knee high boots. Coincidentally my outfit matched Ben's in colour: a bright navy, knee length dress with large black flowers patterned within the material. It was sleeveless with wide shoulder straps, a V-neck and a flattering gathering to the right side of the waist, falling comfortably around my petite pear-shaped figure. My hair was a very short golden blonde pixie cut. Mom loved it and thought I looked like an actual pixie. I was turned in towards her, my arm around her waist. Mom, between us, stood in her light grey 'sweetie wrapper' jumper. Ben called it that because the shoulders and top of the sleeves were embossed with multi-coloured shiny pieces of material that looked like sweetie wrappers. She had paired it with smart black trousers and suede flat lace up shoes. Unlike me and Patricia, mom was apple shaped, much slimmer on the bum, hips and thighs and her 'sweetie wrapper' jumper flatteringly hid the weight around her tummy. Her hair was just slightly longer than mine in a silvery blonde shade. She looked delicious. And though me and Ben were already smiling for the camera, when mom put her arms around our waists and gently pulled us closer, her smile that met her eyes, lit up the room.

I Thought We Had Years

Lauren Love

Chelsea Flower Show May 2018

The train was due in at Birmingham NEC at quarter past one. I parked in the short stay, walked over to the entrance, up the escalator and stood waiting for ten minutes or so when I heard them before I saw them.

"I told you not to buy so much" travelled mom's unimpressed voice.

"You're such a know all" Patricia retorted in a sisterly tone. They just managed to squeeze through one of the ticket barrier aisles, each with a large bag in one hand, and an even larger bag resting on top of their small, wheeled suitcases, plants brimming out of the tops of them. This was the ever-entertaining return from the Chelsea Flower Show. I took a bag from each of them and gave them a long hug and kiss.

"You had a good time then?" I said smiling.

I Thought We Had Years

"Oh, it was lovely, it's always lovely, you must come next year, you'd love it" enthused Patricia.

I had been with them many years ago with nan Lucy, after grandad Henry had passed away. Nan Lucy was not impressed with the lack of available seats to rest awhile. Mom had taken that baton and ran with it ever since.

Every year she got the train there with Patricia. They stayed one, sometimes two nights in a nearby Bed and Breakfast and got a taxi to the show. After walking around the gardens while keeping an eye out for Monty Don, who reminded them of their dad Henry in mannerisms and stature, mom would eventually tire. Then her whole focus was on seeking out a spare seat on a bench, as rare as hens' teeth at this event. Mom could spot a gap on a bench at a hundred paces and those hundred paces were the fastest she walked all day. She would park her bum triumphantly, instructing Patricia to get a cuppa and a sandwich while she saved their sacred seats and watched their bags. Her big sister never questioned why it was always she who fetched the refreshments, quite happy in her role.

This year I had offered to pick them up to save them getting a taxi home, just an excuse to spend time with them really, in between work. We all made our way to the lift as Patricia told me about all the things she had bought, while mom rolled her eyes.

"What did you buy mom?" Her face broke into a big smile and her eyes twinkled as she said,

"I got you a lovely present, I hope you like it."

"Naughty" I said, beaming back at her. Before the lift doors reopened, mom handed me a beautiful shoulder bag with hand embroidered flowers. As we walked outside towards the car park, Patricia was still regaling us with tales of the last two days. Mom was walking ahead, I a few steps behind her, and Patricia trailing behind. This was the usual order of things.

"I was saying to Bern, that was such a fabulous weekend, where could we go next, we need to grab life by the horns, the world is our oyster, what do you think Bern?" asked Patricia brimming over with 'joie de vivre'.

"I just want to go home" mom answered dryly without even a backwards glance. Patricia's enthusiasm was unswayed as she continued with future getaway ideas. We got in the car, and I couldn't stop smiling to myself the whole way home.

I Thought We Had Years

Lauren Love

Holiday of a Lifetime September 2018

Patricia always came up with holiday destination ideas and mom happily went along with it. They had enjoyed trips to Corfu, Ibiza, Gran Canarias, Rome, but Venice was mom's dream destination. She had surprised her sister by suggesting it on their holiday the previous year. Patricia found a package holiday to Lake Garda with day trips to Venice, Verona and the Dolomites. Now they were there.

Mom texted me a few times full of excitement about everything they had seen so far. Patricia said mom was up early every morning unprompted ready for the day's excursion - this was unheard of. Usually, Patricia would be up hours before mom each morning and if mom went to the toilet, Patricia would make her bed while she was in the bathroom. Mom was never very impressed by this.

"Bloody hell, I only went to the loo" she would say as she untucked the covers and climbed back into bed.

When mom came home, I had never seen her so full of excitement to share her holiday stories. She said she had the best milkshake in her life at a café in St Mark's Square; Patricia thought she was mad because it cost fifteen euros.

"I told her you can't take it with you, you know" she said to me shaking her head. They had the best burgers they had ever tasted at a restaurant in Venice, near the moored gondolas. Mom was determined to go on a gondola, but Patricia did not feel steady enough on her feet to get into it, so mom went with a group of other couples, which made me feel a little sad. The most romantic thing to do in the most romantic city in the world and she was on her own.

"I wish I could have known that kind of love in my life-time B"

She said Lake Garda was so beautiful it didn't look real; it was like being on a film set. She told me that every evening they would sit on a wall in the square outside their hotel, drinking hot chocolate, listening to a young man and a girl singing, accompanied by a guitarist. They had a boat trip around the lake and read letters under Juliet's balcony in Verona. This Holiday had clearly made her feel more alive than she ever had before.

"You have to go Lauren; I will take you" she enthused.
"Sounds amazing mom "

"Will you let me take you? I'll pay, you just must go" she insisted

"I would love to go with you mom, but you won't pay."

The following year she insisted again that we go, but that year was Patrick's sixtieth birthday in August, and we had already booked a holiday for it in Cornwall.

"We will go next year mom, you can show me all the places you went, and we can go on a gondola together." "How about September after you get back from Cornwall?" Her persistence was very out of character.

"We can't take that much time off work, so close together mom. I do want to go, it sounds amazing, but Patrick's sixtieth holiday is already booked. We will definitely go next year." I had never seen her so alive talking about this holiday but now she looked deflated, as she sighed and looked away, her face saying, 'It won't happen.' I could not shake the feeling in the pit of my stomach, but subconsciously batted it away as best I could.

I Thought We Had Years

Divorce Request Late 2018

A s soon as I sat down with mom at her dining table, she pushed an envelope towards me with her address on it

"Read that" she said, looking unimpressed. Ben laughed out loud, shouting through from the lounge,

"Oh yeah, read that Lauren, priceless." I opened the letter, it was computer printed, all in capital letters, it was from dad. He wrote that this was his third and final letter to her, that it was obvious 'her' family wanted nothing to do with him, that none of us were there for him when he had gone through very low times, and he felt it was best if they get a divorce but that it would be costly for them both. That was the gist of it, but he lengthened it out with long words that no one would use in daily conversation unless they were in a period drama. The tone of the letter throughout was bitter and angry.

"What are you going to do?" I asked her.

"I will write back and tell him I agree." She wrote a few lines back to him saying she had never received any other letters and yes, a divorce was a good idea. She never heard from him ever again.

A Nagging Feeling 2018

M om and Patricia were going to see the New Year in at Eugene and Louise's house, one of Patricia's son and daughter in laws. They often spent New Year's Eve there with Patricia's daughter, Fleur, and her family too. We never joined them, one, because I didn't like New Year's Eve, always preferring to treat it like any other evening and two, because Patrick had never felt at ease in other people's homes. So, we always did the same thing, early drink in a pub, home with a takeaway by nine, in bed way before midnight. New Year's Day I liked to see mom. I did always feel guilty though as I knew mom would have loved us to have joined them, she would always tell us we had been invited but knew we wouldn't go.

This year she seemed more eager for us all to be together. Just before Patricia was due to pick her up to go, she phoned me reminding me that it would be lovely if we could come. Ben was out and when he came back, he found a note with Eugene's address on it reminding him of the same. Neither of us went as usual. All night I had a nagging feeling, I knew we really should be there. As the New Year dawned, I never allowed myself to dwell on it.

Lauren Love

Puddles January 2019

Patrick wanted a dog, I didn't. His brother and his wife, Joseph and Ann had just bought a Lhasa Apso puppy. Ann sadly realised straight away that she could not cope with him while Joseph was at work, due to her condition, muscular dystrophy. He was the cutest puppy you could ever imagine, so the writing was on the wall. I still tried to dissuade Patrick, explaining that I didn't see how we would be able to spend enough time with him. He said it would be something just for me. I had no idea what he was talking about.

I told mom about my reluctance and asked what she thought.

"I think you should have him" she said suprising me.

"Do you? Why?" I asked.

"Because I know you will love him." She said matter of fact. When someone loves you, really loves you, they can see what you need, even if you can't. Our new fur baby, who we decided to call Puddles, was meant for me, though I didn't know it yet.

I Thought We Had Years

Jaeger Bombs February 2019

It was the day of Patrick's mom's funeral. He was the youngest bar one of ten, so his mom (and his dad before her) had lived to a ripe old age of 95 and 93 respectively. Mom and Patricia were here, and mom who would usually be content to sit at her table, was happy to mingle with me, saying hello to lots of Patrick's family members who she had met over the years. Patricia chatted to anyone and everyone in earshot. As we stood chatting to one of my brothers-in-law, Patrick put his arm around mom and said,

"You'll have to look after me, you're the only mom I've got now." She just looked up at him and smiled shyly. Then she randomly asked,

"What's a jaeger bomb Patrick? "Looking towards a sign behind the bar promoting four of them for £10.

"It's a kind of liqueur that tastes like cough medicine" he replied smiling down at her.

"Do you want one?" she offered.

"No thank you" he said with a little laugh. Patrick was a lager drinker. A little later I was back at the table talking to Patricia when we both wondered where mom was. I glanced around the room, my eyes ending on the bar, the last place I expected to find her. She was paying for four jaeger bombs all lined up, with Patrick and three of his brothers standing beside her. They each reached for their glass, raised it to her, drank it down in one, then looked like they were in a gurning competition as she smiled to herself and walked back to us.

Towards the end of the evening my youngest brother-in-law asked me which one was my mom.

"The one who always looks like she's up to no good" I said rolling my eyes.

"That one" he said pointing straight at her. She smiled over at him, like butter wouldn't melt.

Lauren Love

Erogenous Compost March 2019

All the grove's residents knew and loved mom. They knew her as Bernie. Patrick and I had asked mom to come and live with us in the Isle of Man many times, but she didn't want to leave the grove or the rest of the family. Since I'd been back, I realised just what good friends, her neighbours had become. Mary next door always looked out for her, as did Pam on the other side of the grove. Dina and Jim in the end house had been a real support. Dina ran a craft club every fortnight at the local library and mom found it was something she really enjoyed. On the weeks there was no craft club, Dina invited mom to her house where she would continue her craftwork while they chatted over a cuppa.

Mom had the smallest but prettiest garden, just five-foot square of grass with gnomes, ducks, potted plants, fairy lights and a large shrub in one corner. At the opposing corner was a beautiful flamingo tree which Terry next door had planted for her. Terry was a retired gardener. His first few years on the grove went unnoticed because he kept himself to himself. He lived in the only other flat in the grove, below mom. His front door was unpainted and weathered, his net curtains covering the door's glass panel in need of a wash. When the council were changing all the front doors and modernising the kitchens, Terry was the only one who would not let them in. After the upgrades, his shabby frontage was even more glaring. Mom would always say hello and ask his opinions on her plants when she saw him, and she would often bring his much-loved dog Ringo treats or toys back from her shopping trips. Ben would often come home to find mom playing loud music like an unruly teenager, telling her she should turn it down. This role reversal really tickled me. She carried on regardless as was her way but after Ben had pointed this out a few times, she asked Terry one day,

"When I play music can you hear it?" Terry smiled and said,

"One word Bernadette... headphones."

One spring day in 2016, as I turned into the grove, a bright red door stood out at the far end, next to mom's white upvc door. Gone was the net curtain and the strip of garden under Terry's front window was all freshly dug up. From then on mom and her neighbours got to see a lot more of Terry, often sitting on his garden chair outside his front door with a cuppa with Ringo, a large, long haired lurcher. Ringo sprawled out on mom's garden with his own cup of tea in front of him. Mom and Terry had become good friends, a simple friendship bound by chats about their gardens mostly. I told mom that I thought she had helped Terry out of a depression. She found this hard to believe as she hadn't done anything. I told her she had, just by being her.

It was now 2019 and spring had sprung. Mom had bought a large pink rhododendron and intended to keep it in the pot she had bought it in. Terry told her it would die in the pot. He offered to plant it in her garden but advised her it would do better if planted in ericaceous compost. On entering Wilkinsons with the sole purpose of buying said compost, I stopped to browse some toiletries on offer. Whilst I was mooching, mom said, amidst other shoppers,

"Come on Lauren, we need to find the erogenous compost." I burst out laughing.

"Did you just say erogenous compost?"

"Yes, why what's it called then?" she said none the wiser about my giggles. We headed off to find the compost as I explained the definition of erogenous, a conversation you never think you are going to have with your mom.

Terry planted the rhododendron, and it bloomed as he said it would. About a month or so later, we walked out of her door, heading to do the food shop at Asda. She pulled the door shut, turned, and paused looking at her garden, then pointed at the rhododendron and neighbouring plants. "You gotta watch what these plants get up to in this erogenous soil you know." I linked her arm as we chuckled out of the grove.

I Thought We Had Years

Lauren Love

Good Morning Loveliness May 2019

Ordering her usual three separate portions of six rashers of best back bacon from the deli in Marston Green, the butcher asked,

"Not with your daughter today?" He was used to seeing us together though mom did often go there on her own. He was a rotund, red cheeked man. We liked him. He was always very polite and kind to mom, always walking around to the front of the counter to pass her purchases to her, rather than popping them on top of the counter as he did for most of his customers.

"No, she's shopping in Solihull, she's just phoned me." she told him. After a minute or two of friendly chat between them, mom found herself telling him,

"Do you know, she texts me every day saying Good Morning Loveliness."

"Oh, how sweet." he said pleased that she had confided in him. I loved hearing about this encounter, knowing my daily texts must mean a lot to her if she had told him about them. I sometimes thought she must get fed up with me phoning her so much. I phoned at least twice per day, but always starting and ending the day with the same texts, 'Good morning Loveliness xx' and 'Ni Night, Sweet Dreams xx.' As mom had never been an early riser, I always waited for a text response before the first phone call of the day to make sure I wasn't waking her. The night-time text had gradually become earlier and earlier as she had started going to bed earlier. I thought it was to watch her own programs in bed but when I asked her what she had watched, the bedroom television was seemingly getting switched off earlier and earlier too. Like a lot of things, I registered this change but then shook it off hearing mom's voice in my head telling me,

"You're such a worryguts."

Lauren Love

Mama This One's for You June 2019

en often played a CD called 'Better Than Home'
by Beth Hart. I had never heard of her before but
loved this CD. So of course, the next thing I know,
mom has bought it for me. Her favourite song on it was
'Tell Her You Belong to Me', we both often listened to it
in her flat. I loved this song too, but the CD mom had
bought me was the Deluxe Edition and the bonus track
on it was a song called 'Mama This One's for You'. I
would often listen to it in my car and every time it made
me feel emotional as it was exactly how I felt about mom.
I don't know why but lately I had been playing that song
over and over.

Today we were in the car together and the Beth Hart CD
was in the player. I pressed play and selected the last
song, the bonus track.

"Listen to this song mom, it's how I feel about you."
The song played as I drove, I felt a lump in my throat and
my eyes filled as she listened quietly to the lyrics. When
the song ended, I reached over and held her hand. She
squeezed it, looked at me then quickly looked away. I

realised then how alike we were. We both found it hard to say how we felt, even to each other, even though we were so close, maybe because we were so close. So often mom had put a song on her CD player at home and said, "Listen to this." Then sat on the edge of her small sofa, leaning forwards, listening intently though she had played it hundreds of times before, often miming the words. It had only just struck me that this was her way of opening up to me, telling me how she felt about love, life, me. Now here I was doing the same.

Mama This One's for You by Beth Hart…

For all the things I never said
I'm sorry that I never did
I thank you for your precious time
For teaching me how to climb…
I love you more than summertime
You've been such a good friend of mine
And every sacred word is true
I learned to love because of you and…

Oh mama I saw the world
And it was good
And full of kindness
Every step I took you held my hand
And watched me grow
You'll never know
How much I love you

Lauren Love

And I am not afraid, I'm not afraid
I finally grew
Mama this one's for you…

You always look beyond the dark
You told me joy lives in the heart
And life is what you make of it
Make sure to cherish every bit and…

Oh mama I saw the world
And it was good
And full of kindness
Every step I took you held my hand
And watched me grow
You'll never know
How much I love you
And I am not afraid, I'm not afraid
I finally grew
Mama this one's for you
You, you, you
Mama this one's for you
You, you, you
Mama this one's for you.

I Thought We Had Years

Lauren Love

Too Much Puppy Love 9th July 2019

It was Ben's fifty second birthday and he and mom had come over for a roast dinner. We were still in our one bed flat on the farm with our tiny galley kitchen. I was in and out, checking how the dinner was doing. When I walked back into the lounge, Puddles who was now just eight months old and full of energy, love, and mischief, was trying desperately to get anyone to play with him, going from one to the other. He had clearly decided mom was his favourite, springing up, trying to get onto her lap.

"He loves you mom." Ben said laughing at Puddles' persistence to get to her.

"I wish he didn't" she replied dryly. She looked tired and though she couldn't help but smile at him, he was clearly too boisterous for her, so Patrick picked him up and gave him a cuddle so mom could relax. Mom came into the kitchen to ask if she could help, I told her I was fine, but she stood and chatted while I plated up our meals, asking which was her plate and saying,

"That's enough for me" as each item was apportioned. She had never had a big appetite, so this was normal. When we had finished eating, all plates were empty apart from mom's. It was lovely she had said but she was full. So, I waited a while before serving pudding. Again, mom asked for a small portion and again, she didn't quite eat it all.

A month earlier mom had bought me a mug for my birthday with a picture of Happy Dwarf from Snow White with the words 'Always Happy' on it. At the same time, she had bought one for Patrick's birthday in August with Grumpy Dwarf saying '24/7 Grumpy'. It really tickled mom, she said,

"I don't know how I've got the nerve because he isn't grumpy is he." Later in the evening I made teas and coffees and as I sat down with my cup of tea in my Happy Dwarf mug, mom whispered,

"You will have matching mugs soon" and we both smiled. Mom suggested they should go before it was even nine o'clock saying I had to be up so early for my work shift at the gym the next morning. Typical mom thinking about everyone else all the time.

I could tell she had really enjoyed the evening, she loved me and Ben being together as we hadn't been in each other's lives much until he lived with her. So, her lack of appetite, the tired look in her eyes and her early departure were filed to the back of my mind under 'worryguts' as we all kissed and hugged goodnight and Puddles in my arms, managed finally to get a crafty lick of her ears.

I Thought We Had Years

Lauren Love

Poldark 14th July 2019

I hadn't seen Mom yesterday like I usually did because we had been on a friend's birthday outing. I hated missing our day together and had intended to go and see her today, though I hadn't told her that. My stepson Sabin was coming over for dinner, so, I was going to pop to moms for an hour on the way to picking him up. Just as I was getting ready to leave, one of my brothers-in-law, Richard, rang to say he was nearby and could he pop in. Richard was a good egg, and we hadn't seen him for a while. It was good to see him, and I didn't want to rush off as soon as he'd arrived. So, I decided not to go to mom's, knowing she wasn't expecting me.

That evening, having just dropped Sabin home, I made a rare hands-free phone call to mom, on the way back. I had timed it so that I would be back home to watch Poldark at nine o'clock. Me and mom were big fans. It was the first TV program in ages that we really looked forward to each week and nothing could interfere with our viewing. As soon as each episode finished, I would phone her, and as soon as she picked up, she would say,

"Well … good stuff eh" and we would then discuss all the best bits. Mom's were always any that involved a topless Poldark and his love scenes. The difference in her voice was so slight I could have imagined it when she said,

"So, you have just dropped Sabin off?"

"Yes, I'm heading home in time for Poldark now. Why? Are you ok?"

"Just wondered. Yes I'm fine." She sounded tired, worried maybe, I couldn't put my finger on it. I almost turned the car around and headed to her, but I didn't.

In a few weeks' time I would convince myself that, the sound in her voice I could not recognise was pain and fear.

Lauren Love

Angel of Death 30th July 2019

Six monthly blood tests were another thing mom had to have, in addition to her four weekly depixol injection. Depixol adversely affected kidney function and so the blood tests monitored this. She had her routine blood test four weeks ago. During our shopping trips these last two weeks, mom had used the toilets in Asda and each toilet trip was longer than the norm, in fact she never normally used the public toilets at all. When I asked her if she had diarrhoea, she said, with irritation,

"You know I'm prone to it," which she had been over the years on and off due to side effects of medication. She received a letter asking her to go for another blood test. Mom was not happy about this, she hated having the blood tests and thought she wouldn't have to go for another six months but I could see she was worried too.

I convinced her to let me go with her to the doctors to see if they could give her anything for her upset tummy and to ask about the extra blood test request. It proved impossible to see a doctor, so we had to settle for a nurse.

The nurse was very thorough, asking umpteen questions and feeling her tummy. She looked at mom's details on her computer screen and said that mom's tummy bug may have affected her blood test, hence the request for another one. For this reason, she advised mom to leave it four weeks before she had her follow up blood test, so that the tummy bug would be cleared up. Not knowing any better, this made sense to us and I for one, felt a wave of relief rush over me. I marked on my calendar to take her to Solihull hospital for a walk-in blood test (a much more pleasant experience than at the doctors) in four weeks' time, Tuesday 30th July.

When we were next in Asda mom said did I mind if we just got her shopping and went home. I would usually get a bit of shopping for myself too. She lingered in the Asda toilets again. As she was reaching for ham in the chilled aisle I said,

"Mom, I really think you should have that blood test as soon as possible. I know you are prone to diarrhoea, but you shouldn't have it for this long."

"I know, I think there might be something seriously wrong" she said looking away from me, seemingly checking the use by date on the ham.

"Right, we will take your shopping home. I will put it away and then we will go to Solihull to get your blood test" I said trying to hide the worry in my voice.

"No, we will go on 30th July" she said abruptly.

"But that's still a week and a half away mom, why do you want to wait that long?"

"Because that's what the nurse said" she insisted.

"But if your tummy bug doesn't clear up it won't make any difference" I persisted gently

"30th July" she repeated and that was the end of it. She was as stubborn as a mule at the best of times, you could never sway her from doing what she wanted, it was something I loved about her usually, but today I wished she would back down just this once.

A week later mom asked if I would get her shopping. She stayed home. This was not good, mom loved shopping. After unpacking it, we sat at her dining table with a cup of tea. She was her usual smiley self, pleased to see me, happy that her food cupboards were full again. But as we chatted, I looked at her little face and it was quite literally littler. I had been so busy doing her shopping, helping her with bits of housework that it was only now, today, as I sat in front of her, that it hit me how much older she suddenly looked. I didn't tell her. When I got home, I told Patrick. He reminded me that she was seventy-one now and I felt reassured because I so desperately wanted to be.

It felt like time had gone into slow motion until Tuesday 30th July arrived. I let myself into mom's flat and heard nothing. Not the usual, 'Hello dumpling' or 'Baby' She was sat on the edge of her small sofa and all she said to me when I walked in the room was,

"Hello, angel of death." It was so out of character, I laughed and said,

"Oh charming."

Mom hardly said a word until the nurse announced, smiling at her,

"All done" mom hadn't flinched

"You were so gentle, thank you" mom said to her, as her face broke into a smile for the first time that day. In my ever-optimistic mind, this told me that mom had been worried about having the blood test done, rather than what the results would reveal. So, my face finally broke into a smile too.

As we were leaving the hospital mom asked if we could go to Marks and Spencer's in Solihull for a bit of posh food shopping. As we walked into the store, she turned to me and said,

"Can we be in and out today Lauren?"

"Yes of course" I said thinking all the worrying about the blood test must have taken it out of her. We walked back towards the car park, me carrying mom's two heavy carrier bags. I was normally very strong given my job, but I had injured my arm and so kept stopping and switching hands. Mom insisted on carrying one of them, but we ended up compromising by both of us holding one handle each of the carrier bag that was on my injured side. I was deliberately taking most of the weight but trying to make mom feel better by helping me. After about a dozen steps, mom said she felt sick. I took the bag handle from her, and her nausea passed. We were almost at the car and once we were back in her flat, sorting through her goodies, she said she felt ok again.

The next morning as I was getting ready for work, an unknown number flashed up on my mobile phone

"Hello" I answered.

"Hello, is this Lauren Love?"

"Speaking."

"Lauren, it's Marston green surgery. We have your mom's blood test results back. Can you bring her back in to us to go through them?" Mom's doctors had always had my number as next of kin, but they had never called me before.

"Yes, ok I will let mom know and get her to call you to make an appointment" still not grasping it.

"She needs to come in today, can you bring her?"

"… yes … what time?"

"Nine thirty?" the doctor offered. It had only just turned eight thirty, it would be tight, and mom would not appreciate such an early appointment, forcing her out of bed. So, I asked for a later appointment and settled for eleven thirty, phoned mom, she reacted the same as me. I had tried so many times to get her to the doctors, now neither of us wanted to go.

I Thought We Had Years

Lauren Love

Cancer Pathway 31st July 2019

Me and mom were sat in front of a locum doctor, I can't remember her name, but I will never forget her face. She said lots of things but the only parts I remember were,

"Bernadette, your blood test result shows a protein that needs further investigation so I will be referring you for a consultation at Solihull hospital" She asked Mom no questions, not one.

"In the meantime, are there any lifestyle changes mom should make that will help?" I asked, oblivious to the optimism of my question. She didn't answer for a few seconds, she simply shook her head.

"No, there is something going on here and we need to get to the bottom of it." Mom hadn't spoken a word.

"You will receive a letter with your consultation date in the next week, if you do not receive it in the next week, phone us to let us know." As we started to rise out of our chairs, she added, looking at mom, "I must tell you that you are now on the cancer pathway." I was now catching up with mom, I felt numb, muted, though my head had a million questions. I opened the door and mom stepped out ahead of me, I then unbelievably and selfishly turned back and quietly asked,

"I am going on holiday in a week's time, should I go?"

"Where are you going?" she asked.

"Ilfracombe for a week" I answered.

"If you're in this country you can always come back" she said. As we walked the few steps to the car mom said solemnly,

"I've got cancer, I knew it."

"That's not what she said mom, they always put people on the cancer pathway to fast track you, so you get your consultation sooner, so they can rule it out sooner rather than later" I reassured her, believing every word because I needed to, because the alternative was unthinkable. Mom just kept looking at her hands in her lap, not wanting to say anything to burst my irritatingly optimistic bubble. During the five-minute drive back to her flat, she asked with the voice of a child,

"How will I get to the consultation; you will be away?"

"We don't know when your appointment will be yet mom, we will sort it out, don't worry." As I write this, I break my own heart all over again, wishing I could go back in time to shake myself out of my denial, my selfishness. Our impending holiday was for Patrick's sixtieth birthday, I didn't want to let him down and selfishly, I was starting to feel like I needed it, ready for what was looking likely to be a tough time for mom when I returned. I wasn't in complete denial, there was clearly something wrong with her. I would be refreshed and stronger for her. Ben would be home with her. Patricia was supposed to be away too at her own caravan but said she would cancel it as she could go there any time. She was always there for me and mom, and I was more grateful than ever right now. It would all be ok. This was my logic.

Back at mom's flat I asked her if she had been in pain for a while and not told us, she nodded very slightly as she turned to me with her head dipped, eyes looking up at me.

"Where is the pain?" I asked her. She placed both hands on each side of her lower abdomen. "What sort of pain is it? Sharp or a dull ache?" I continued.

"It's like period pain but worse" she said.

A few days later I was cleaning at the farm, as Hilda, my boss chatted to me. My phone rang and I excused myself telling her it was mom. Hilda had met mom and really liked her, always giving her a big hug.

"My appointment has come through Lauren, its Wednesday 14th" Mom sounded anxious, scared even. Instantly I registered that it was smack bang in the middle of our holiday week, and she knew it too.

"Ok, well Patricia said she wants to go with you, Ben will drive you both there." I said calmly while my heart was beating through my chest. "And then I will be home on the Friday, and I will be with you for any appointments you need after that, ok?" A quiet

"mm" was all I heard down the phone. The panic in my chest was rising and I found myself reluctantly asking

"Would you rather I take you?"

"Yes "

"Why's that?" I gently asked her.

"Don't know."

"Ok mom try not to worry, we will sort something out, I'll phone you back in an hour after work." The instant the call ended, I burst into a sob that I couldn't contain and ran out of the cottage.

"Whatever's the matter?" Hilda's concerned voice followed me down the stairs. I couldn't speak, I just kept running. I sat in my car outside until my sobs subsided. I phoned Patrick and told him I didn't know what to do. He suggested we get a train back from Ilfracombe on the morning of mom's appointment and a train back there on the afternoon. Usually, his suggestions or different perspective would help me see things more clearly when I couldn't see the wood for the trees. But not this time. All I could see were the trees and they were closing in on me as each day passed.

Hindsight is not a wonderful thing; it is just a stick to beat yourself with. Mom didn't need my logic, my optimism, or my strength, all she needed was to hear me say I would be there. The next day her usual response text was one word missing, reading, 'Morning loveliness.' She told me later she couldn't bring herself to put the word 'good' in front of it.

Lauren Love

Motherhood 3rd August 2019

Today was one of my brothers-in-law, Joseph's seventieth birthday, Puddles' first dad. Patrick was full of a cold, so I attended the birthday bash at Joseph's local pub on my own. Their niece was there with her three-week-old baby daughter, Winny. Obviously, I had to have a squidge and somebody took a photo of me holding her.

When I left, I went over to see how mom was. Mom had said many times, in a cheerful, complimentary way,

"You would make a lovely mom" to which I replied,

"Babies are lovely, but even lovelier when you can hand them back." I showed her the photo that had just been taken on my phone. She looked so sad as she looked up at me and said,

"You would have made a lovely mom." I was forty-eight now, so she obviously thought another grandchild highly unlikely, but the change in her words from,

"Would make" to "Would have made" hung in the air and I could not get them out of my head.

I Thought We Had Years

Self-Preservation 7th August 2019

Yesterday while I was with mom for our usual Tuesday together, I asked her if she was any worse and did she want to go to the doctors. She said she was ok and showed no interest in going to see the doctor again. This morning as I was heading out to work, Ben texted me saying mom wanted to go to the doctors, but he was tied up with work so could I take her. I phoned her and said I would come straight over and book her an appointment before I left. She told me not to, that she could go on her own because I had to go to work. I told her I would be straight over. I phoned the doctors and even after explaining the details of mom's last appointment, could only get to see a nurse. I cancelled my daytime classes, leaving just my evening class to do, then headed over to mom.

I Thought We Had Years

"Why do you want to go to the doctors today mom? Yesterday you said you didn't want to go" I asked gently. Her answer floored me.

"I can't stand the pain anymore." The nurse again was very thorough, she looked at her blood test results on her screen, asked lots of questions and asked her to lie on the examining table so she could feel around her tummy. Mom got on and off the table with ease. This was a good sign the nurse assured us. She asked mom where the pain was, mom indicated with her hands both sides of her lower abdomen.

"Mom said it feels like period pain but much worse" I added. Mom's tummy was soft, again this was a good sign she assured us.

"If it was anything sinister, the tummy would feel bloated and hard" she informed us. This was all so good to hear but I was still on red alert. Mom was still in pain. The nurse said to take paracetamol to ease the pain until her consultation in one week's time.

"If we didn't get any joy with you today, I was going to take mom to A&E" I told the nurse "And I still think I should because she is in so much pain. She is not one to complain usually." The nurse suggested that A&E would tell us the same things she had and that we would be waiting for hours, suggesting mom would be better in the comfort of her own home. I wish I had been stronger for her. I normally was I thought, but panic was rising in me, and I had never felt so uncertain of the right thing to do. The nurse's words had relieved me, but mom was in pain, and I wanted somebody to wave a magic wand and make that pain go away. As we walked back into the grove, mom holding my arm, Terry was sat outside his door with Ringo.

"Oh no" mom whispered

"You go in mom, and I will explain to him you're not well." Mom gave Terry a quick smile and walked straight past Ringo, to open her front door. I quickly told him the dilemma about whether to go to A&E. He thought a lot of mom, they had become good friends, he looked really concerned then finally said,

"She doesn't look good, maybe you should go to A&E" Then I told him about Patrick's special birthday holiday and how I did not know whether I should go. "That's a tough one" he said, "you have to live your own life too." I settled mom on the sofa, she said she didn't know what she wanted to do, we decided to stay home.

I popped to Asda to get her some complan as she had no appetite. As I walked down the aisles I phoned Patricia, still desperately waiting for someone to tell me the right thing to do. She reassured me that I should go on my holiday because Ben was with mom and while he was at work, she would go around to check on her. When I got back to mom, I made up the complan, she sat up to drink it, telling me it was delicious. She drank it all. She was the loveliest patient, eager to let me know I was doing a good job of looking after her.

"Thank you for dropping everything for me Lauren" she said weakly.

"It's only work mom, you're much more important." She Smiled at that. I gave her a couple of paracetamols and a glass of water.

We were due to go to Ilfracombe the next morning and I'm ashamed to say I needed tomorrow to come around quickly. I was struggling. I told mom I had spoken to Patricia, and I was going to make sure she checked on her every day.

"Don't you dare" she said in a heartbeat.

"Why not?" I asked took aback.

"I'm fine, if I need her, I will call her" she insisted.

"Ok" I surrendered. Hearing her say she didn't need Patricia to come around each day made me feel relieved, maybe I had been worrying too much after all.

"You had better get off, you need to get to your night class" she said as she gently snuggled back down into the sofa in the foetal position. I leant over her, and she reached up to give me the tightest hug she ever had. This was another joke between us. I would normally wrap both arms around her and she would just put one arm loosely around me, I would then say,

"Call that a hug" she would grin cheekily and put her other arm around me and give me a gentle hug. But not today, both arms were wrapped tight around me for much longer than normal and as our embrace ended, she said something that should have made me listen to my gut rather than anyone else's advice, something she had never said to me before.

"Miss you already." I covered her with a blanket, headed downstairs to let myself out and as I stood in her porch about to close the door there was a moment when the world seemed to stand still, a moment when I very nearly went back up to her, but I didn't.

Word to the wise, if your world stands still, there's a reason for it. I kept telling myself she had Ben and Patricia, that I would be back in a week, building my wall of self-preservation higher and higher.

I Thought We Had Years

Lauren Love

Consultation 14th August 2019

I had spoken to Patricia and texted Ben several times while we were on holiday. I couldn't get any response from mom. They said she seemed ok, no worse. Mom phoned me twice, the first time on Saturday morning to say happy birthday to Patrick. She sounded so quiet, like talking was zapping all her energy. Then said she had to go because she had made herself a coffee, like making herself a coffee was a major event too. The second time she called was on Monday evening when we were in a pub waiting for our meal. I excused myself from the table to talk to her, she sounded the same as she had on Saturday. I asked her how she was feeling, was the pain any worse, she said it was the same. I told her I missed her and after her consultation in a couple of days we would know what was causing her pain and they could start making her better, she was nearly there. And I would be home a couple of days after, on the Friday. I was doing most of the talking. Patrick came over to me, stroked my arm and told me my meal was going cold. I asked mom if I could call her back after I'd had my meal, but she said she would be in bed, this was about eight o'clock. I returned to the table. Patrick had eaten half of his meal and I had lost my appetite.

On Wednesday morning, the day of mom's consultation, I sat in the bay window of our holiday apartment, looking out at the sea, in need of nature's calming effect as I phoned her. This time she answered.

"Morning mom."

"Hi Lauren" she said weakly or sleepily, maybe both.

"Is Patricia with you yet?" I asked just as I heard my auntie's voice in the background calling,

"Come on Bern, it's time to get up." Patricia had already told me a few days before that if the consultant sent mom home rather than admitting her to hospital, then mom could stay with her, and she would look after her.

"Listen mom, if the doctor today sends you home, let Patricia take you back to her house. She wants to look after you and I think you should let her."

"I should go home with Patricia? she repeated as a question back to me.

"Yes, I think you should."

"Ok Lauren" she said so quietly. I felt a little stronger, maybe due to the ebb and flow of the sea, maybe because Patricia had taken the reins, maybe simply because I liked talking to mom and she was agreeing to my suggestions, no longer stubborn.

Patricia helped mom to shower. Mom had told me a week ago she struggled to shower due to the pain, I offered to help her shower, she shook her head. I think she was trying to make me realise how serious this was. I think it was another subtle way of hoping I would want to stay of my own volition rather than her ask me to stay. Ben drove them both to the consultation at Solihull Hospital. Ben waited in the car park. The consultant examined mom's bowels and said he could feel something there that would need further investigation. He would refer her for an MRI scan. He was sending her home. Patricia said surely her sister would be better off in hospital, she would not take her back home still in pain just to wait for yet another appointment. The consultant said they could go to Accident and Emergency, but he could not admit her to hospital without the MRI results. As they walked away from the doctor's office, mom holding her sister's arm, Patricia felt a hand on her shoulder. She turned to see the nurse who had been in the consultation room with them.

"Take her to Heartlands A and E, not here." Moments later I was talking on the phone to a handsfree Ben, Patricia, and mom, though mom never said a word. Ben and Patricia were talking over each other telling me what had happened: Ben saying Patricia should have left mom there, then they would have had to admit her, Patricia saying I'm not leaving her on her own, no way, Ben not understanding why she wanted to take her to Heartlands when they were already at Solihull, Patricia repeating what the nurse had said. I was stood against a building in the middle of the town near our holiday apartment in Hele Bay, I turned, wondering where Patrick had gone. He was pacing up and down a side alleyway, glancing over at me and then back at the floor.

"What does mom think?" I asked.

"She's on death's door Lauren" shouted Ben's voice full of panic.

"Right, take her to Heartlands." I instructed with a confidence that came out of nowhere.

"Ok, we'll let you know what happens Lauren." said Patricia. The call ended as I turned to Patrick who was now by my side, looking very solemn.

"You ok?" I asked as I held his hand. He pulled me towards him and held me tight.

"I'm just worried about your mom" he whispered into my ear. I had spent the last couple of weeks feeling a total mess, a hopeless, indecisive, panic-ridden mess, while everyone around me said what I needed to hear, that it would be ok. The tide was turning. Mom was going to hospital, they had to admit her, the consultant said she needed an MRI, they would give her pain relief, scans, they would give her the treatment she needed, she would be in safe hands now, they would make her better. I felt like a pillar of strength, while Ben, Patricia, and Patrick started to crumble around me.

"I think we should go home first thing tomorrow morning" Patrick said. I agreed, feeling my newfound strength growing stronger still, in the knowledge that I would be back with her in just over twelve hours.

First Day in Hospital 15th August 2019

We drove to collect Puddles from his holiday home with Joseph and Ann and to collect my car which we had left there. I headed straight to Heartlands hospital and Patrick took Puddles home. As I walked down the hospital corridors carrying the seaside gnome for mom, I saw Patricia ahead of me. She seemed back to her normal self, not the stressed lady I heard on the phone yesterday. No doubt relieved that her sister was finally admitted at midnight last night. Tired but relieved. I should not have left her to deal with this by herself.

Mom was sitting on the edge of the furthest bed on the ward, next to the window, looking towards us. She looked like a rabbit caught in headlights.

"I thought you weren't back until tomorrow" were the first words she said to me.

"We came back a day early, I wanted to see you" I told her. When Mom was admitted last night, they said they would be giving her an MRI scan today. Patricia went to check what time that was likely to be.

"I'm glad you've brought Patricia because she doesn't like parking" mom reminded me.

"No, we've come separately mom, I caught up with her walking to the ward."

"Oh", she said. I asked if she was in less pain now as I reached my hand out to gently touch her tummy.

"Don't Lauren" she said quietly, answering my question. I showed her the gnome. She ran her finger slowly down him, from his nose to his toes.

"He's nice" then handed him back to me saying, "Take him home." Patricia went home after a few hours. It was almost four o'clock now so I asked when mom would be having her MRI scan. The nurses at the ward desk did not know but after chasing it up, told me that an emergency had come in, pushing mom's slot to tomorrow. Mom was on morphine. I hated seeing her suffering, but I was still positive and relieved that she was now in the best place. She had pain relief and tomorrow's scan would tell us more so they could start to treat her. The nurses were so kind and gentle with mom, one male nurse in particular called Bobby, I could see mom liked him. When I went home that night, I knew she was in good hands.

Lauren Love

Impossible Choice 16th August 2019

The MRI scan was due at two o'clock. I was with mom as visiting started at ten in the morning. Ben was working, and I had kept him informed of what was going on mostly by text. He found it hard to see her in pain and told me,

"She'll be alright now, they'll fix her." Mom kept changing position looking uncomfortable. Every time she switched from lying on her back to sitting up to lying on her side, I would gently wrap my arms around her shoulders to help her reposition herself and each time she would hold me for what felt like a precious eternity. There was so much I was saying to her in my head but I had no voice, nothing would come out and I knew she felt the same. Nurses came again to take more blood tests, this time from the back of her hand, saying it was a different blood test and it was not a nice one, another nurse holding her other hand. My muteness extended to the nurses, I never asked them what the blood test was for, I trusted they were doing what they had to do. I felt useless but I was there now and that was all that mattered to both of us At twenty to two, twenty minutes before the MRI scan was due, a young man and young woman sat themselves near the foot of mom's bed while I stayed seated by her side. They introduced themselves to her, they were doctors. They both placed their hands gently on her arms and never took their eyes off her, not looking at me once. I liked that, mom was the patient.

"Bernadette I'm afraid the blood tests have shown that you do have cancer." I couldn't take it in, I wasn't expecting to hear what was wrong with mom until after the scan, how could they just saunter in like that and hit us with it. Mom was lying slightly on her left side towards me, not looking at me or the doctors, just fixing her stare mid-air.

"The dilemma we have," they continued still leaning in towards her "is that your kidney function is only fifty per-cent and the contrast dye we must use in the MRI scan reduces kidney function further. The scan will tell us what type of cancer it is. Without the scan we cannot treat you, if need be, you would have dialysis." Everything was snowballing, mom's expression did not change, I felt like I had been punched in the stomach. Mom looked beyond exhausted.

"What would you like to do Bernadette? It's your deci-sion." Some decision, I felt like screaming, but my mouth was still muted until I finally said,

"What do you think mom?"

"I suppose I'd better have it done" she said quietly, still gazing mid-air.

"I think that's the right choice, then they can start giving you treatment" I said, not knowing whether it was. All I could hear in my head over and over were the words 'cancer' and 'dialysis,' some choice. Two o'clock came and a male nurse I hadn't seen before pushed mom in a wheelchair to another department, while I guided the tall pole on wheels that held her intravenous fluids. As soon as mom was taken in, I was texting Patricia and Ben to update them and then phoned Patrick. I could not be left alone with my own thoughts; I needed him to keep talking to me until mom came out.

Later that afternoon, a different male doctor came to mom's bedside. Again, he was kind and spoke gently.

"I am sorry Bernadette, but the MRI scan has revealed you have ovarian cancer." He gave us a moment to absorb his words. "The mass is about this big" indicating the size of two hotdogs side by side, with his hands.

"Which side is it on?" I have no idea why I asked that, but I needed to know what was happening inside her, I needed to picture it.

"The tumour is on your right ovary" he said to mom. Her hand involuntarily passed over her right lower abdomen.

Later that afternoon just after Patricia arrived, a female doctor appeared at mom's bedside, introducing herself as a gynaecological doctor. All I remember hearing was,

"We will move you to the gynaecological ward, then we will do this, then this ..." She had a plan. she could treat the cancer. Patricia felt positive too after hearing the doctors plan of action. Mom's next visitor was Bobby. He told her that they needed to fit her with a catheter as her bladder wasn't emptying on its own. He asked if she would prefer to wait until a female nurse was free. Mom shook her head. He asked if she wanted an anaesthetic applied first, I was repeating his questions to her in case she couldn't hear him, she nodded. I held her hand tight and stroked her brow saying,

"We want all the anaesthetic we can get, don't we mom" I smiled softly, wishing she didn't have to be messed with so much. Hadn't she been messed with enough all through her life.

Later that evening after Patricia had gone home, mom was sat in a chair on the right-hand side of her bed, looking out of the window. The curtain between us and the next bed had been pulled over, I don't know if it was for our privacy or the other patient's, but I was glad of it. Without taking her eyes away from the window she broke the quietness.

"I've got ovarian cancer" she said to herself.

"Yes, you have mom, but they are going to treat it. They are going to make you better."

"No, I'm too far gone" she said still looking out of the window "I'm dying." Her words shrank me from a forty-eight-year-old to a five-year-old.

"Well, you can't and that's all there is to it, because … what will I do?" were the strange words that finally came out of my mouth. She turned and looked at me.

"I don't know." That was the moment every shred of optimism, every ounce of hope drained out of me as we held each other's gaze, her eyes crying out that she was not ready to leave me. Finally accepting what she had known for some time, what the rest of us would not even consider. She had let us hold onto our hope, knowing we needed it. She had struggled alone until this moment.

There was no small talk, there was no big talk, I did not tell her how much I loved her, nor she I. We knew.

Later that evening, mom was back in bed, lying slightly turned on her right side towards me as I sat in the chair by the window. Hours had passed quietly. As I looked at her, she looked so serene. I thought how scared she must be. I thought how badly I had let her down when she needed me most. I wondered how much pain she was in and how much pain she had been in last week, at home while I was on holiday.

"What are you thinking?" I asked.

"I'm thinking how beautiful you are" she smiled.

"Well, we know where I get that from don't we." She shook her head. She never ceased to amaze me. Even now, serenity and love shone from her.

A while after that, time now had no meaning, moms breathing became very laboured and they placed an oxygen mask over her face. All I knew was Ben was coming at eight o'clock. Mom sat up, moved the mask away from her mouth and managed to get three words out "Don't forget Ben."

"I won't mom, I've spoken to him, he's coming at eight." She put the mask back on, and slightly shook her head, just once, exasperated. I knew exactly what she meant but couldn't acknowledge it even now, so I busily tidied her bedside table instead of telling her what she needed to hear. As Ben arrived and I left, I asked the nurse at the ward desk to call me if mom worsened at all during the night and I left her to time alone with her son.

239

I Thought We Had Years

Lauren Love

Not Coming Home 17th August 2019

A s soon as visiting started, I walked onto the ward to find the curtain drawn around mom. As I reached the foot of her bed there was a gap in the curtain through which I saw Bobby and four other nurses, maybe a doctor, I don't know, just a worrying amount of medical people around her.

"Your daughter's here Bernadette" Bobby said to her while holding her hand. Mom looked over at me. I felt like the rabbit trapped in headlights now, but I hoped my face was hiding it as mom looked at me. I wasn't sure what they were doing, it looked like they were taking blood but why so many of them? I felt myself crumbling, breathing deeply, trying to pull myself together.

They were all surrounding her again a couple of hours later. The bell for end of visiting rang and Bobby looked over at me and mouthed,

"You can stay." That floored me. I had to walk off the ward for a few minutes. I phoned Patrick who was working. We knew that Patricia was coming in the afternoon, but Patrick suggested I call her and ask if she could come sooner. For the first time I felt my ability to stay strong for mom slipping away fast. Then I phoned Patrick again to say Patricia was coming. While I was still on the phone to him, I felt an arm slip around my waist she was here. I told her how worried I was about mom getting so much attention from the nurses and doctors and thanked her for coming so quickly, but she remained unfalteringly positive. Metaphorically we were walking in line, in our usual order: Mom had been steps ahead of us for the past few weeks at least, I was reluctantly catching up and Patricia's faith allowed her the luxury of trailing behind.

That afternoon a doctor asked us to join him in his office.

"Your mom, your sister, Bernadette" he said as he looked at each of us in turn, "is a very poorly woman. The cancer has spread to her lungs and other parts of her abdomen. I'm so sorry, she won't be leaving here … she won't be coming home." He was only telling me what mom already had, so it should have come as more of a shock to Patricia. Yet I crumpled, sobbing so hard I could barely breath as my auntie held me.

"Can I stay overnight with her" I eventually asked.

"You need to go home and rest so you can stay strong for her" he said, and Patricia agreed with a nod.

"Are you going to tell her now?" I asked him.

"We don't normally, but you can tell her if you think that's best" he replied. Patricia looked at me uncertain.

"She already knows" I told her.

I Thought We Had Years

Lauren Love

Holding On 18th August 2019

My phone rang at half past three in the morning, my heart was thumping out of my chest.
"Lauren?"
"Yes" I said jumping up and grabbing my clothes.
"Your mom is ok, but she has become a little more uncomfortable so as you asked me to call you …"
"I'll be straight there." Patrick was already pulling on his jeans. As he drove, I called Ben and Patricia. We all arrived just after four o'clock. The curtains were drawn along the side of her bed.
"We came to see you mom because the nurse said you weren't feeling very well." I said as I kissed her, still not wanting to cause panic. She was unable to talk now, her breathing laboured even with the oxygen mask. She was frail but her legs were swollen. Two hours later the other patients started to wake.

"How's Bernie doing?" I heard one of the other patients ask and a few other concerned murmurs. She had only been here three days and there was obviously a lot of concern for her. Ben said he needed to phone into work and would be back later, he looked ashen. As Patrick and Patricia sat near the foot of the bed, mom kept changing position, unable to get comfortable, like before, every time she tried to sit up, I wrapped my arms around her back, to ease her up onto the edge of the bed, she wrapped her arms around me so tight and for so long, our hearts breaking, until I eased her back down onto the bed. Patrick also went to sort out work later that morning.

For the rest of that day mom had a constant queue of visitors. First Louis, Patricia's eldest, who took his mom back to his house for lunch and a rest when he realised she had been there since the early hours. She didn't want to leave us but then her other two sons Eugene and Tom arrived, so she kissed mom on the cheek, telling her she'd be back later. By this time mom had turned away from her visitors, towards me and closed her eyes. Next up was Jack and Nina, mom's grandson, and his ex-girlfriend. Mom always hoped they might get back together. I'm sure it perked her up a little, as she turned to lie on her back again. Leigh and Michael, her granddaughter and partner were just minutes behind. Shortly after Dawn (Jack and Leigh's mom) and her other two other daughters Maryam and Aminah arrived so I gave mom a kiss and let them all have some time with her. As I was sat in the waiting area outside the ward, Leigh came out to tell me they were moving mom to a room of her own, the first room on the right as you entered the ward. I knew this wasn't a good sign but told myself it was to give mom and all her visitors more space and privacy. It's odd what goes through your head in traumatic situations, the nonsensical things you do and say, the things that will forever be unsaid, undone. Patrick came back, John and James arrived (mom's cousins). Patrick left me to show them to mom's room, which prompted the other seven members of family to head home. Mom looked much worse, how long had passed? I had no idea.

"Can you hear us Dette?" asked John and I realised that was the first time anyone had spoken to 'her' for hours. James placed a large ornament of an owl on her bedside table, double checking with me that,

"She does love owls doesn't she?" Only a few minutes later my friend Ellen walked in. Patrick had asked her if she could be there for me. John and James insisted they should go, signalling for me to follow them out for a moment. They both loved mom very much and had kept it together for a few minutes by her bedside, but now outside the door, James was sobbing, and John's words snapped me out of the fog I was still in.

"I'm sorry bab, I can't watch someone die." I walked back in the room, nowhere to turn now. I wanted to lie by her side on the bed, but I didn't want to hurt her, so I sat by her left side because she was turned towards that way. I held her hand, it was curled into a half fist and so cold, I stroked her face, kissed her cheek, I had no words. Ellen was reminiscing but her voice was muffled, like she was somewhere in the distance. Ben walked in the room.

"Ben's here mom" I said holding her hand. Ellen left the room and just a few moments later as the two people she loved most in the world each held one of her hands, she began to snatch her breath. I reached my left hand over to hold onto Ben's hand, holding hers.

"We'll look after each other mom, won't we Ben?" I couldn't take my eyes off her but saw through the side of my eye Ben's bottom lip trembling.

"Yes" he quivered, as I returned my hand to hers and stroked her brow.

"You rest now mom, you rest now." She took her final breath. It was three minutes past five in the afternoon. She had waited for us both to be there and she had heard all she needed to hear.

Lauren Love

Brought Up Properly Moments Later

Ben stood frozen to the spot, I walked around the bed to him, pushing my arms under his jacket, wrapping them around him, burying my face in his chest,

"What are we going to do without her?" I cried

"God knows" Ben said holding me tight. When we let go of each other we stood looking at her in a trance.

" We are so lucky, she's the best mom in the world" I said to him standing by my side while I stroked her arm.

"One hundred percent," said Ben. He told her he loved her and kissed her forehead I couldn't bear to say goodbye, so I said my usual

"Ni night, sweet dreams mom" Then Ben couldn't get out of there quick enough, saying he was going to Leigh's. I phoned Patrick. I couldn't say it. I didn't need to. I asked him to let Patricia know. She had been there for her little sister all her life from the moment she was born, her rock. She would be broken that she hadn't got back in time. A nurse approached me, with condolences and paperwork. I told her how lovely all the staff had been with mom and thanked her with what was left of my shattered heart. A few moments passed with the nurse's mouth moving without me hearing her words until she randomly said,

"Your mom has obviously brought you up properly, she will be very proud." It seemed like the least likely thing someone would say after someone has just died, but it was perfect. I looked upwards and smiled, hoping mom was in between worlds, knowing she'd be thrilled at what she had just heard.

Lauren Love

I Thought We Had Years
17th September 2019

Mom had told me many things regarding 'getting her house in order' before anything happened to her: where her file of paperwork was, listing who she paid bills to; she told me what songs she would like played at her funeral; where she would like her ashes laid. This trickle of information started in 2017 when she was sixty-nine, prompting me to ask,

"Is there anything wrong mom, you would tell me if there was, wouldn't you?"

"No, I'm fine, but I'm nearly seventy you know, and you never know what might happen once you've turned seventy" she said chirpily. I reminded her that nan and May both lived well into their eighties, so she had good genes, to which she just smiled. I believe for a good eighteen months before she died, she knew something wasn't right, she felt her body slowing down. Maybe on a good day she put it down to getting older, but I'm pretty sure on a bad day she was scared. Yet somehow, she made our suffering as short lived as possible by keeping her own suffering to herself. Her selflessness in dying, as in living takes my breath away. I felt I had failed her, that I hadn't listened, really listened. Ben said we were blindsided as her symptoms were not dissimilar to the side effects of her medication, so we did not see them.

As I sat in the front pew of Woodlands Chapel, comforted by Patrick and Patricia either side of me, Ben stood reading the eulogy he had written. It was perfect, I was so proud of him, and boy would she have been. I wish I'd had the strength to stand beside him and read the poem I had written for her, but I knew I didn't. I turned to look behind me to see every seat in the chapel filled and the back wall covered with people standing. She had no idea how many lives she had touched. Still hoping there was an 'in between worlds' I whispered to her in my head,

"Look how loved you are." Ben returned to the front pew nestled between his son and daughter. I felt rooted to my seat as Louis, Patricia's eldest son, approached the front of the church to read words that had poured out of me on paper, but I could not utter.

Lauren Love

I Thought We Had Years …

I thought we had years …
Years of walking arm in arm in the park.
Singing 'Busy Doing Nothing' and 'Truly Scrumptious,'
A little too loud perhaps.
Sitting on Carrier bags on wet benches.
To keep our bums dry.
Curling up on your sofa, for cosy cuddles and naps.

I thought we had years …
Years of sending silly texts each day to make each other
smile,
Talking nonsense on the phone
"What do you two find to talk about?" Patrick would say.
Checking my watch before I call,
So I don't clash with 'Neighbours' or 'Home and Away'

I thought we had years …
Years of listening to Daniel O'Donnell at Richter scale ten!
Ben playing you up for doing him that 'big spread'
His home cooked meals on your table,
But sometimes you just wanting a sandwich instead.

I thought we had years …
Years of your face lighting up,
Finding the perfect gift, the perfect card,
For our birthdays or Christmas, or just because.
Carefully wrapping; which tag? which bow?
Because it matters, it really does.

I Thought We Had Years

I thought we had years …
What will Patricia do?
Us three musketeers are now only two.
Cinema outings, the tea dance and tai chai
Are of no interest without you,
To her or to me.

I thought we had years …
Years more of the good stuff to make up for the bad.
So afraid and alone inside your own head,
Battling what you call "The Invisible Worm"
So brave, so selfless and my helpless love.
Of real pain, real love, from you I did learn.

I thought we had years …
Years of You.
Kind, Beautiful, Cheeky You.
I can feel your long, tight hugs in those last few days.
You knew soon I'd be broken and lost,
So held me close to carry me through the pain.

I thought we had years …
How can they be snatched away so suddenly?
Our love, so strong, so rare for all to see.
I can't shake myself awake from this heart-breaking dream.
Since you're gone, my love for you is killing me.

Lauren Love

A Lost Friend
7 Months Later, March 2020

I stood in the grove with Puddles. I placed one of mom's gnomes under her pink flamingo tree. Terry next door had dug it up and replanted it in the communal central grassed area for all the neighbours to remember her by Today would have been her seventy second birthday. I knocked on Terry's door, thinking how strange it was that two of his large plant pots were knocked over. It hadn't been windy overnight, and he would have picked them up when he walked Ringo that morning. There was no answer and my gut told me something was wrong. But standing outside his door, right next to mom's, wishing more than anything in the world that it would open, and she would step out of it, in her Paddington coat one more time, I realised I shouldn't have come here. I walked to my car and as soon as I got inside the floodgates opened. Moments passed, my tears subsided, and I phoned Terry, it went to voicemail. I told him I hoped he was okay and thanked him for replanting mom's tree and for just being a good friend to her. My words became choked as the tears returned and I ended the call. Less than an hour after getting home, mom's other neighbour Pam flashed up on my phone.

"Lauren, it's Pam from the grove. I thought you'd want to know; Terry has passed away." I felt winded. He had been found lying on the floor by his bed with Ringo by his side. Mom's other next door neighbour Mary had called the council to enter his property, as her concerns grew. He had suffered a heart attack that morning on mom's birthday. Mary and Pam said he had lost weight and gone downhill ever since mom passed away.

"He has taken it really badly." Mary had told me just after Christmas. I remembered him telling me how much he missed her, that their friendship was very simple but very rare. I thought back to a day when they were stood chatting as me and mom were heading out to the shops. The youngest family in the grove walked out of their house, three-year-old Oscar running over to wrap his arms around mom's legs shouting,

"Hello Bernie" then mom saying to Oscar's dad

"Ooh nice beard Adrian."

"Oh Bernadette, you and your beards" Terry laughed.

Condolence cards are a kind gesture but for me they merged into a blur of platitudes. The only one I remember was Terry's. The words he wrote were not for us, but for her. The words I could not bear to say, even now, even to my own heart...

"'Goodbye Bernadette, my Friend.'"

Lauren Love

Quiet Strength The Next Day

I hadn't slept all night, thinking about Terry, thinking about how many lives mom had touched. People told me so many stories about mom when I asked them to share their memories of her for this book. One friend of the family who always struggled for money, told me how mom had given her £100 every summer towards her children's school uniforms. Another friend of the family told me how mom would often take him lunch while he was working in his shop, knowing he usually didn't get chance to have a lunch break. Her neighbours told me how she would always buy their children a little something at Christmas. Dawn told me when she and Ben were first going out together, Ben would sneak her into his bedroom, dad would throw them out and mom would wait up and let them back in after dad had fallen asleep.

Aminah told me her nan Bern would always visit her and her sister Maryam near their birthdays to bring their present, always bringing an extra present so the other sister would not feel left out. Mom would try to give Dawn petrol money when she insisted on driving her home. Dawn would never take it, but she often found a £20 note stashed away in her handbag days later. All these things we had never known, came as no surprise.

It suddenly occurred to me that mom was born in '48 which was my age when she died, and I was born in '71 which was her age when she died. I don't know what made me think of that or why it brought me comfort, as though even in death we were linked. I suppose I was just playing with numbers still. That night I wrote her one more poem, slid it into a clear plastic sleeve, rolled it into a scroll and tied a pink ribbon around it.

Today I could feel the promise of Spring in the air as I sat cross legged on the grass in front of mom's headstone. I took the scroll out of my bag, kissed it and placed it snugly under the two-inch gap below the base. Then for the first time, read my poem out loud to her, with fingers crossed on both hands that she was listening.

Lauren Love

Quiet Strength

7 months, 1 day and 16 hours without you,
Without your strength that held us up.
Suddenly crippled,
Stumbling through each day,
Without your Love that spread like ripples.

That gentle kindness in your eyes,
Your words were few and heartaches hidden,
But you were always there
And boy could you listen.

Auden's poem is a reality,
Someone has stopped all the clocks.
There's a lesson to be learned here,
But I can't seem to join the dots.

I pray to a God I want to believe in,
That finally you understand,
We weren't your 'rock' or 'guardian angel,'
For it was *You* who held *our* hand.

I Thought We Had Years

Lauren Love

Legacy of Love September 2022

Today is the day I write this final chapter, three years, two weeks, and four days after mom died. Mom told me, "Don't ever change." But the death, especially the sudden death of someone who is at the very heart of your own being, does change you, how can it not. For a long time, I felt rooted, like the world was still spinning around me but I was unable to move, unable to move on.

They say grief is love that has nowhere to go. Patrick was right about Puddles. He was my reason to get out of bed every morning for a very long time. He licked my salty tears dry and snuggled up to me when the waves of shock, regret and grief crashed over me time and time again. He was just there by my side. I had never noticed before how his character is so like mom's; stubborn, cheeky, mischievous, sleepy, and so loving. In him I feel I still have a little piece of her.

Patrick struggled, not knowing what to do or say. He felt like he had lost me for a while, but he hadn't. I needed him more than anyone, more than ever. Just like mom, I

261

was in a cocoon, no-one could get in and I could not get out and it was so lonely in there. In time, Patrick learned from Puddles' example and realised, I just needed him to be there, by my side.

Ben and I are closer than we've ever been. He said he feels like the ready brek kid with a warm glow around him, not because of eating porridge like the advert, but from her love. She is within him.

Patricia is our roots now. She thinks we are being kind when we go to see her. As life is short, I put her straight and told her we need her more than ever now.

It has been an emotional journey but one I selfishly had to take. On every page, I've felt mom's hand reaching out to mine, leading me through each moment. The sense of achievement is immense. I wrote this book to give mom a voice, a voice I felt she did not have for so long. It is my way of saying sorry to her. Sorry for not being there when she needed me most in her last week at home, a sorry that will last forever.

She was a very private person and so many times I've questioned whether she would want anyone else to read it. Then I remind myself of her words …

"Everyone has a book inside them waiting to come out"

She was simply too extraordinary to keep quiet about. Her legacy of love too great a blessing not to be shared.

For my part, when I stopped mourning her and started listening to her, I let that love in and she saved me.

Lauren Love

Where Are They Now?

Patricia? … her world is very different without her sister and best friend. But she continues to enjoy her retirement, doting on her grandchildren who love staying with her because there are no rules. She has just started going back to the tea dances and tai chai.

Ben? … I'm sure his world is the most changed. He could not bear to stay at mom's flat, he said he was always looking for her in those rooms. He moved out to his own place and the grove residents felt this as a double blow as he was their last link to their friend Bernie. Every Christmas, he raises a glass to mom, with Jack, Leigh, Dawn, Aminah and Maryam, as they sing along to Barry Manilow's 'Can't Smile Without You.'

Puddles? … he is now the involuntary receiver of all my love for mom, often looking at me as if to say, 'Oh no, not another cuddle.'

Patrick? … he misses the banter his mother-in-law always lined up for him. He talks about her often which I love him even more for.

Ringo? ... he lives with Mary, mom's next-door neighbour, along with her husband, two teenage children and their other much smaller dog. They did find another owner for him. On the day he was collected, he refused to leave the grove, lying down on mom's small patch of garden, near the end of Mary's front path. Mary and her family love their gentle giant Ringo with all their hearts and would not be without him.

Me? ... I am changed. This is a new chapter in my life, and I intend to show mom I will make the most of every page.

And Bernadette? ... some say she is often on the angel's naughty step, creating mischief wherever she goes; some say she is sat on a bench in a beautiful garden with Terry having a natter; some say she is with her mom, dad, and May having the catch up of all catch ups; ...but in her spare time I know exactly where she is ... with me of course, always.

Acknowledgements

The biggest thankyou to my ever-patient husband Patrick, for allowing me to hog the laptop for the last two and a half years without even a roll of the eyes. For encouraging me to just keep writing in my many moments of doubt.

Thank you to Ben for telling me to write fearlessly, advice which made me push on through the hardest parts of this story, even when those hardest parts took him on a difficult journey too.

Thank you to Patricia for being unflinchingly convinced that anything I write will be absolutely fabulous!

Thank you to Ro for her ongoing support.

Thank you to Talia, for volunteering to be my PR and fan club manager before I'd even finished the book, keeping my positive pants well and truly pulled up!

Thank you to all the beta readers for their time and feedback which made me realise I was on the right track.

Thank you to Rose for her kindness and expertise as voluntary editor. I cried happy tears when she told me the book revealed how extraordinary mom was. Everything I learned from her was invaluable and allowed me to give the book a 'good polish'.'

Thankyou to the authors of 'sociallyshared.co.uk' for their advice, inspiration and for making me feel part of their fabulous group, supporting and promoting local women authors.

Thank you to Puddles for keeping my feet warm during the many hours spent writing.

Thank you to my mom and cherished friend, Bernadette for teaching me to see the world with kinder eyes, cheeky humour, and love… and of course for the notebooks. "

Printed in Great Britain
by Amazon

14857579R00161